MOODS OF
FUTURE JOYS

around the world by bike
PART ONE
FROM ENGLAND TO SOUTH AFRICA

ALASTAIR

HUMPHREYS

Published by
Eye Books Ltd
29 Barrow Street
Much Wenlock
Shropshire
TF13 6EN

www.eye-books.com

First published in Great Britain 2007
Second edition 2014

Cover design by Dan Armstrong

The events and opinions in this book originate from the author. The publisher accepts no responsibility for their accuracy.

British Library Cataloguing in Publication Data.
A catalogue record for this book is available from the British Library.

Printed by CPI Group (UK) Ltd, Croydon CR0 4YY

ISBN: 978-1-903070-85-7

Foreword

Sir Ranulph Fiennes, OBE

Alastair Humphreys' expedition was out of the ordinary.

In today's world of dashing up Everest in less than a day, sailing round the world in 10 weeks, and best-selling books about three-month motorbike rides, Alastair's journey stands out as amazing. It was probably the first great adventure of the new Millennium.

This journey was an old-fashioned expedition: long, lonely, low-budget and spontaneous. It was a life on the road rather than a whirlwind break from home.

An expedition lasting four years requires tremendous persistence, flexibility and self-discipline. To cycle, mostly alone, so many thousands of miles down the lonely roads of some of the world's wildest regions demands great strength and toughness – mental as well as physical.

When Alastair's carefully prepared plans to ride through Central Asia to Australia collapsed, he would have been forgiven had he shrugged his shoulders at the tough luck, given up and returned home to have a go at something else. But to change his route so drastically, to turn spontaneously and ride instead through the Middle East and Africa showed enormous determination, lateral thinking and a love for life and for adventure.

He aimed high, minimised his risks as best he could, and then leapt in with enthusiasm, trusting to the general good nature of mankind to help him through. The reward was an impressive circumnavigation of the planet crossing five continents that a journey! Alastair certainly did not take easy options on his journey (a winter in Siberia, a summer in the desert of Turkmenistan are examples) and this of course made success all the sweeter.

Alastair set himself a ferocious challenge, an old-fashioned quest, and got on his bike to see how hard he could push himself, what he could endure, how far he could go. He must be proud of pulling it off, against the odds and against the doubts of so many.

I am sure Alastair learned a great deal, about the world, about himself, during the often lonely weeks and months and years of hard work. This expedition demonstrated that all things are possible if you work hard enough to achieve them. I would like to congratulate Alastair on his impressive accomplishment and wish him the very best of luck with his future exploits.

Contents

Yorkshire to Cape Town

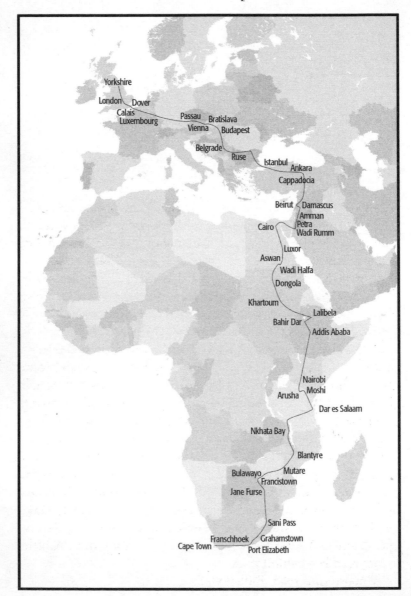

The Road Ahead

All that you are experiencing now,
will become moods of future joys,
so bless it all.
– Ben Okri

Days are long on the road. Pack up and pedal into the dawn. Ride until sunset. It's easy to kill time but you can kill distance only by riding. Roads roll on forever, linking and connecting and reaching so far ahead that to think about the end is to think of something that feels impossible. So settle for today, for earning the small distance that the day's long hours will allow you. Roads drenched with rain, stinging hail, pulsing heat, slick ice, buffeted by winds on loose gravel, deep sand, tangled rocks, thick snow. Roads of smooth tarmac down mountainsides on sunny days with warm tailwinds and scenes of impossible beauty. Roads furious with traffic through grim slums, bland scrub, concrete jungles, polluted industrial wastelands. Monotony in motion. Roads too hard and too long that break you, expose you, scorn you, and would laugh at you if they cared. Roads too hard and too long that you pick yourself up from, have a word with yourself, and make it to an end you once doubted. Roads you have never ridden to places you have never seen and people you have never met. Days end. A different sunset, a different resting point, a different perspective. A little less road waits for you tomorrow. A little more road lies behind you.

Choose your road. Ride it well.

For my vast support team of strangers, who became friends.

If you're not hurting you're not riding hard enough.
If you're not hungry you've eaten too much.
If you're not cold you're carrying too many clothes.
If you know you will succeed it's too easy.

Beginning

My journey begins. The bags are packed, my head is shaved (a 'new beginning' type thing) and I can think of no convincing excuse to back out. I am trapped on a runaway train that I set in motion myself but now am powerless to stop. I don't want to do this. I wake up feeling physically sick with fear. I can't do this. I roll out of my bed for he last time, open my curtains for the last time and look at my beautiful view of the Yorkshire Dales for the last time. I realise that if I take stock of all these 'last times' then I will be in floods of tears before I even make it downstairs (for the last time). I have to do this. I focus my efforts on smiling for the sake of my parents. Everything seems surreal. Is this really happening to me? I don't have to do this, do I? I stuff a tin-foiled pack of sandwiches into my panniers as if I was heading out on a jolly day trip, awkwardly wheel my heavy, cumbersome bike out of the garage, wait while Dad asks the neighbour to take a final family photo, hug everyone goodbye, and I am off. As easy as that. I have crossed my first border: from dreaming of a big journey to being somebody who is on that journey.

The start is inauspicious. After 50 metres my mother yells at me for forgetting my helmet and I have to trudge back to the garage for it. I then realise that, despite the months of research into mountain roads of the Andes and Sudanese border crossings, I have no idea which road to take out of my village. So I guess. I guess wrong. And my father shouts, and points me right.

Finally, I round the corner, my home is gone and it all hits me. The mounting pressure and months of denial all explode inside me, and I burst into tears. I have just left from my front door to try to cycle around the planet. I have left behind everyone that I love. If I was a brave man I would turn around right now. Go home. Go home, and admit that it was all too frightening. Instead I keep pedalling.

What on earth are you doing, Al? You bloody idiot.

This is one of the worst moments of my life.

Short on Boldness

Whatever you do, or dream you can, begin it.
Boldness has genius, power, and magic in it.
Johann Wolfgang von Goethe

In order to ease myself in gently, and to say some more goodbyes, I stayed with friends along the way through England to Dover. By the end of the first day the face-punch of reality had kicked in. I was knackered. This was going to be difficult in every way. I spent the first night at my friend Richard's house in Cheshire after a less-than-gentle 85-mile debut day. I could barely eat, because of the nervous turmoil in my belly. After dinner I leant back in my chair, listened to one of his father's corny jokes, rubbed the unfamiliar texture of my shaved head, and felt like I was on a runaway train, unstoppable and out of control, yet I did not feel strong enough to hang on.

The next hundred miles to the home of a friend in Worcestershire was better, although it was hardly the gentle warm-up I hoped for. The last couple of months had been a blur of organisation and farewell parties, and no time for exercise. A group of friends gathered for a barbecue. Duncan managed to inflict himself with food poisoning and as I said goodbye to his prostrate form, I wished that it had been me. After one of his Mum's legendary fried breakfasts I was back in the saddle and the end of England was drawing nearer.

A sedate couple on racing bicycles asked me where I was heading on my fully loaded mountain bike. I couldn't bring myself to say 'Australia' as I had no faith that I was going to make it that far. I felt a fraud. I said 'Oxford,' and they were impressed. I wanted to go home. August sunshine danced through the trees and bees hummed their busy way. Families drove past, enjoying the warm day together. Huddles of friendly cows peered at me over the taut fences.

I wound my way through the traffic-jammed London labyrinth to Ziggy's home. My friend Ziggy was also leaving England in a few days to teach in the Botswanan bush for three years. He was having a large farewell party. I had chosen not to have a fanfare departure: perhaps I was thinking of a likely ignominious early return. With my loaded bike, which I had christened Rita, propped in the garden, people raved about my trip, but for once their incredulity struck home. Needing some space I climbed onto the roof of the house and looked over the orange haze of night-time London. Noisy laughter rose from the garden below, with the usual chatter about work, TV, gossip and a little drunken philosophising. I tried to remind myself that this comfortable swaddling was what I wanted to get away from.

I left Ziggy's house to a roar of thunder. Heavy grey clouds choked London and uncaring cars carved waves of rainwater over me. I cried my way out of London to Sevenoaks, a feeble 30 miles, before taking refuge with Arno, another friend from Oxford and the most English of all Frenchmen. I phoned Sarah from a chipped red phone box and desperately wanted to see her. But I knew now how much I really loved her, and that I would quit if I saw her again.

I delayed for a day, enjoying watching England destroy Germany 5-1 in a qualifying match for the 2002 World Cup. Morale began to rise a little; how could it not after that game? Once I left Arno's I had no excuse to linger more. It was time to get going. Leaving England was a huge psychological barrier that I was very reluctant to cross, although I hoped that once I did it things would begin to appear rosier. On my last morning in England I made a conscious effort to keep my head up, to drink in details. If things went to plan I would not see her again for a very long time though I would surely think of home every day. The smallest, most mundane aspects of England would all seem fresh and new, yet welcomingly familiar when next I saw them.

I spent a long night in Dover's ferry port trying to find a comfortable position on a row of plastic seats with a ridge between each person's allocated individual buttock space. Throughout the night a recorded message piped up every couple of minutes, '*Bing, bong, bing, bong:* we would like to politely remind you that the parking zone outside is restricted to 10 minutes only. Thank you. *Bing, bong, bing, bong:* we would like to politely remind you that this is a no-smoking terminal. Thank you. *Bing, bong, bing, bong:* we would like to politely remind you that we have no intention of letting you get any sleep whatsoever on those special uncomfortable seats. Thank you.'

The ferry crossing was grim. The Great British Public were delighted that the bar was open at 7am and were boisterously enjoying shouting about how much lager they were going to drink before reaching Frog-land. I cycled out of the cavernous loading bay of the ferry and I was in France. The journey of a lifetime was underway and all I wanted to do was go home.

But I soon began enjoying being abroad. It is always an exciting sensation. I was due to meet a friend, Chris, in about a week's time in Luxembourg. He was leaving England a few days after me so I would ride slowly until he caught up with me and then we would ride together for a while. I left a graffitied message on a road sign for him saying that I was looking forward to seeing him again. I needed the company. My bike felt heavy, loaded with front and rear panniers and a large dry-bag bungeed on top of the rear rack. I had enough clothes to endure the Iranian winter, camping and cooking gear, spare parts, a spare tyre, tools, a Leatherman and enough books to fill a small library. I was carrying the SAS Survival Handbook (with manly plans that never materialised of catching my own food and navigating by the stars), a Book of Facts (to educate myself), a mini world Atlas (to plot and dream), a Teach Yourself to Draw book (my new project), a mini dictionary of quotations (for inspiration), the latest Harry Potter and the brick-like Penguin History of the World. A little excessive, perhaps, especially considering that I had not brought any underwear to save some weight.

I rode through the killing fields of the First World War around Arras. Half-remembered snatches of poems came back to me, as I reflected sadly on the mad history of those peaceful green fields.

'He's a cheery old card, grunted Harry to Jack as they marched up to Arras with rifle and pack. But he did for them both with his plan of attack...'

'...the rifle's rapid rattle stutters out its hasty orisons...'

'... the old lie...'

The next day was my best so far. I only cried for a couple of minutes in the morning; things were improving. It was starting to sink in that I was actually doing it. I had actually left home with the pure purpose of making this journey. Nominally I had a goal but in reality I didn't. I would travel until I didn't want to anymore, until I had cured my wanderlust, until I had learned enough for now, suffered enough for now, tested myself enough for now and done all the things that this journey demanded of me, for now. Whether or not I could make it right round the world wasn't as important to me any more as having actually taken the first big step. I had learned already that the journey is the reward, and that the destination is purely for others.

The transition to the Euro was just months away and so my mother had given me all her long-hoarded European coins to spend. I decided on a little detour to Belgium for some retail therapy. It was about 10 kilometres out of my way to the first café across the border. I slapped down my cash on the counter, confident of burgers and coffee. When the smiling girl had removed all the out-of-date coins there was still a respectable little pile of coinage. I asked for as much food as I could buy. She handed me a can of Coke and three small chocolate bars and scooped my coins into the till. A little disappointed at my booty I turned around and pedalled back to France. Oh well. I sang to the cows, "I'm the king of the world: I've got a can of Coke and three chocolate bars." It was dehydrated chicken noodle soup for dinner but this time with chocolate for dessert. I was learning to be grateful for small rewards.

I had no map as I was still harbouring romantic notions of ambling unfettered across the globe. The novelty of being lost had not yet worn thin. Surprisingly, given our organisational skills, both Chris and I arrived in Luxembourg on the prearranged day. It was good to see him again. Chris was the friend of a friend and we had met the year before when the three of us cycled across South America. Chris looks like a dreadlocked Harry Potter, but beneath his slight frame lies a steel core and a foolish sense of humour. He was going to ride with me to Istanbul.

Summer was fading into autumn. Toes and noses stung in the crisp dawns. I enjoyed the sight of the World's Fattest Moped Rider, cheerfully straddling his tiny machine with his legs sticking out, the tyres squashed flat and the engine screaming in protest. Lilac crocuses filled a wet meadow and brown cows crunched them in the rain. The rain fell, day after day. My feet turned white and wrinkly being permanently wet for so long. One day as we ate jam sandwiches on a pavement we looked jealously at a table of girls eating huge burgers in a restaurant. Burgers were beyond our budgets.

One ordinary wet morning we cycled with a bike shop owner who was out on his morning training ride. He had caught us up and slowed down to ride with us. He led us at a cracking pace down winding little cycle tracks and shortcuts.

He didn't speak any English and Chris spoke no German so I translated as well as my school-level German would allow:

"I think that he just said that an aeroplane crashed into the World Trade Centre in New York yesterday…."

It was September 12th 2001.

The next couple of weeks seem peculiar now with the perspective of hindsight. The whole world was frantic, like ants in a damaged nest. The repercussions from the terrorist attacks rushed across the world, waves that continue to wash over us all today. Meanwhile, on the banks of the Danube, Chris and I were cycling to Budapest. We were angered and saddened by the attacks, and anxious and unsure about their implications, but it was hard to feel connected with the world, our world, while we were riding through a country where we knew no-one and no-one knew us and the road was stunning and the sun shone and the river flowed peacefully. Sunshine did not feel appropriate to how we felt we should be feeling.

Days rolled by through densely wooded valleys and beneath striking outcrops of rock, perched with churches and castles. There were lots of middle-aged cyclists ambling along in ludicrous shell suits and ill-fitting lycra. Some cyclists would pass us twice, firstly on their ride out and then again later on their way back home. I too was heading for home but I was not planning on turning around to get there. A man in a purple cycling outfit and cycling helmet was standing at a bar, beer in one hand, cigarette in the other. I imagined him leaving home and calling out to his wife, "Right darling; I'm off out cycling now." "Oh well done!" she would have cooed, impressed at her athletic hubby.

As we followed the river, autumn tightened her grip on the year and my evening swims became ever more vocal. As night fell we would relax beside our campfire and cook noodles. With chocolate biscuits to follow, the living was easy. It was a run of glorious days and some of the most beautiful cycling I had known. Lit by crisp sunlight, the colours of the Danube gorge were amazing: deep blue sky, deep green forests, occasional trees starting to burn with autumn colours, bright green crop fields and the golden shimmering Danube. Clean white houses with red tile roofs crowded round the clean-lined churches with straight and sharp spires or curvaceous cupolas. The bike path veered wildly through head-high maize and dazzling oil seed rape and back along the riverbank. Fallen leaves on the track, clickety clack, clickety clack, my own commuter track. Where was I going? Home, I supposed.

Early in the morning the sun rose through white mist as we broke camp. Skeins of swans spanked the water as they struggled to take off. Beams of light carved through the clouds. It was easy to imagine a God. A daub of yellow woodpecker battered at the silence and a snake slithered across the path ahead of us. Tiny villages welcomed cycle-tourers with guesthouses and restaurants. I hoped to return and ride that route again one day when I could afford coffee and cake in all the little cafés. After this ride, I reflected, people would ask, "Did you see Macchu Pichu, the Grand Canyon, the Pyramids?" And I would say, "Yes, and I also saw the Danube."

We pinched apples from a laden orchard, stuffed our panniers and anticipated stomach cramps. It was a surprise to discover that Austria completely shut down on Sundays. We ran out of apples and were famished. It was raining again too. The only shops open were petrol stations and they were too expensive for us so we just kept on riding into and then right out the other side of Vienna in search of an open grocery store. Is my memory of Vienna a unique one, of rain, grey wet motorway underpasses, tower blocks and closed shops?

After Vienna it really began to pour. We were soaked to the skin. We looked for a sheltered campsite, an old barn perhaps, but were turned away from the two farms we asked permission at. That would be the only time of the whole journey that I was ever turned away. We could not find anywhere to sleep and eventually the road left Austria and we entered Slovakia in the dark and camped under a motorway flyover. We lit a fire to warm ourselves but were spotted by a patrol of rifle-wielding policemen. I was nervous as they walked towards us. But they merely motioned to us that they thought we were a bit mad, and that we really shouldn't be sleeping there. However as the weather was so awful they would let us stay where we were so long as we disappeared early in the morning.

Morning meant that yesterday was gone and we grabbed at it early. The rain had stopped. We emerged through the morning fog into Bratislava, a city that immediately appealed. Compared to Austria the relative poverty of Slovakia was apparent in the cars and clothes of the people. A combination of not really eating the previous day and Slovakia's favourable exchange rate led to some serious eating whilst the city sat quietly beneath a cold quilt of mist. A brass plaque set into a pavement told me that I still had 1,200 kilometres to travel to reach Istanbul and 15,000 more to Sydney.

We camped early that evening to dry everything out. With gear spread over the field drying and steaming in the sunshine I studied my new map. I had had enough of wandering free/ being lost. From foul to fair: yesterday we had been cold, wet, hungry and slept uneasily in a place we did not feel safe. Today we lazed in a safe campsite enjoying the sunshine, jam sandwiches and coffee. It made me realise that if I had a tough day I must just keep persevering and eventually things would come good again.

Crossing the river and the border into Hungary we rode past enormous factory complexes brown with rust, decaying and crumbling. In the fields alongside the factories farmers scythed clover and we debated the difference between a scythe and a sickle. Old ladies in thick nylon hosiery picked wild mushrooms, their old bicycles leant against apple trees. We arrived in Budapest and paid for accommodation and a hot shower for the first time in a month. It was a chance for me to wash my intensely smelly and itchy feet. We abandoned the bikes in the hostel and headed out to eat, a feast of traditional Hungarian food: an all-you-can-eat Chinese buffet and a litre tub of ice cream each.

The next day I walked to the British Embassy where the newspapers painted a very black picture for my projected progress into Asia. The Taliban were refusing to hand over Bin Laden and war in Afghanistan was looming. I decided that I could not bury my head in the sand any longer and began considering the possibility of having to detour round Central Asia.

Grime-streaked workers in their overalls stood at high tables in a gloomy market eating spicy sausage and potatoes with their fingers. I joined them, trying to get my head round the options available to me in this new post-September 11th world. Chris too was wrestling with tough choices. He had decided not to go home after Istanbul. He had an Australian passport and he wanted to go and study there. Now he just needed to tell his girlfriend. I knew how he felt...

Hungary's Great Plain was flat to the horizon over acres of vegetables. Bent bodies were hard at work picking paprika and harvesting potatoes and corncobs. We endured evil mosquitoes and then we were into Serbia and Montenegro. The cars were now Yugos rather than Skodas, the drivers hooted at us more and people waved more often. We encountered the first real signs of rural poverty in Europe, tiny dwellings with chickens scratching around outside. The smallholdings and vegetable gardens suggested subsistence living rather than food surpluses and EU subsidies. It felt very different to the Europe we had left behind. There were a few small vineyards and ladies sat beside the road with bunches of grapes for sale. We passed a town that seemed devoted entirely to selling moulded plastic products; rainbows of stacked plastic bathtubs and washing-up bowls. Old ladies in head shawls watched the world go by and hoped for customers.

Two thousand miles from home now and Belgrade was blanketed in a thick, cosy blanket of fumes. It felt somehow comforting and soothing in the rush hour chaos. Wandering the streets of Belgrade we saw postcard sellers with cards depicting Serbia as a final stronghold against American world domination. Celebratory cards of the September 11th attacks also showed an anti-US sentiment. Sadly, over the next few years on the road, I saw this sentiment blooming worldwide.

Belgrade comfortably won the prize for the most beautiful women of the ride so far. Tourists were still something of a rarity and we discovered with joy that if we stopped in the street, with map and puzzled expression, then within moments a blonde beauty would stop to shepherd us in the right direction.

We enjoyed Serbia's autumnal forests, huge hills, limestone cliffs and the gleaming river (littered with plastic bottles). We asked for water at a hilltop farm overlooking the Danube and Romania. The family invited us onto their patio for very strong coffee and a couple of glasses of homemade apple schnapps. As the schnapps warmed our bellies an old man began jabbing his podgy finger at us and saying, "Bin Laden – BOOM, George Bush – BOOM, Yugoslavia – BOOM, Tony Blair – BOOM." Having known war so recently he felt an affinity with what was brewing in Afghanistan.

Romania felt poorer than the other countries we had ridden through so far, with horse drawn carts, barefoot people carrying buckets of water from the wells, kids begging and rubbing their tummies in gestures of hunger and men asking us for cigarettes. We rode past several wedding and funeral processions in Romania. Both kinds of parade featured jaunty music, singing in the street, and homemade wine slugged from bottles. It was hard at first sight to know whether it was a wedding or a funeral that we were passing. Should I ring my bell and wave gaily or nod gravely and look sombre?

Kids wielded peashooters and crossbows made from maize stalks. A teenage boy tried to impress his girl by racing through a village on his horse and cart with her holding tight to his waist and shrieking in delighted terror. The towns had derelict, broken-windowed, rusting factories, but some were still belching out smoke. Large arterial pipelines led to and from the factories, often running between a family's house and their garden or along a pavement. Train tracks across the road faded into the fields, a reminder of Communism's shortcomings and the economic vacuum that followed its collapse.

On our first night in Bulgaria we bid a final farewell to the Danube. It lay old, slow and golden in the setting sun. Factories and darkness framed the river. We said a fond goodbye and headed for the hills. Bulgaria's rolling hills were a pleasant change from the tedious plains of Romania. They reminded me a little of England. An old lady gave us peppers and grapes from her garden and we learned that in Bulgaria nodding your head means 'no' whereas shaking it from side to side means 'yes'.

On and on we pedalled; camping in woods and behind hillocks, buying food in dim and dusty village shops, filling water bottles at petrol stations and village pumps. We were growing fit and strong and our minds were hardening to the long hours on the road each day. I was beginning to grasp that this was the lifestyle I had committed myself to for the next few years or for as long as I could handle it. I was learning to adapt to the routine of the hours and days and weeks that, combined together, ease you slowly across countries and continents.

After a long, painful mountain climb we crossed into Turkey and saw the first signpost for Istanbul, the end of Europe. We slept in a prohibited military zone that night but we didn't care, we were exhausted. Minarets of mosques called the faithful to prayer. '*Allah-u-akhbar*...! God is Great...!' My plan to race across Europe, to get as far away from all that held me there before it sucked me back like a magnetic field was working. I felt generally happy and I was now a continent away from home.

The lure of a bed overcame any sense of foolishness as we raced into Istanbul after dark down a terrifying motorway. Predictably enough we were caught by the police. A little less predictably, the police allowed us to continue on the busy motorway and helped us with directions. Racing afraid down a busy motorway was an unusual arrival at the gateway to Asia. I had crossed my first continent. I was 4,500 kilometres from home. It had been a sad, unexpectedly difficult farewell and beginning to my ride. The journey had definitely begun, but would it be able to continue? The world seemed poised to go crazy and I now had some big decisions to make about where I could go next.

The Single Step

The longest journey starts with a single step.
Lao Tse

It was an exciting time of life. Leaving university with the world laid out before me, I was at the junction of a number of paths, unable to see far ahead but with a hazy picture of where each may take me.

Knowing that one road ultimately leads to another, I knew that I would never come back. It was time to choose. So I chose to leave everything that I was familiar with, everything that I knew and loved and enjoyed. I turned down a good job. I chose to leave my friends and family, my girlfriend and my country.

I decided to let go of everything that makes life normal, secure and conventionally happy. Like the movie poster in my student halls, I chose not to, 'choose a big television, choose fixed-interest mortgage repayments, choose a starter home, choose sitting on the couch watching mind-numbing, spirit-crushing game shows.' I chose something else. I was tremendously excited by life, and didn't think I would find it where I was. I knew that leaving would be hard, but, like Candide: 'I should like to know which is worse, to be raped a hundred times by negro pirates, to have a buttock cut off, to run the gauntlet among the Bulgarians, to be whipped and flogged in an *auto-da-fé*, to be dissected, to row in a galley, in short to endure all the miseries through which we have passed, or to remain here doing nothing?'

It is a greedy, ungrateful risk to give up everything that makes you happy in the hope that you can find something better. You risk not finding it. You risk finding it and then never being satisfied again, always yearning for more. But I was looking for experiences that nothing, not the dimming light of old age nor financial ruin, could take away from me. Uncertain travel held an appeal for me, a luring magic, an intoxicating release from conventional bonds, a chance for self-testing and self-discovery, and the rushing joy of being alive that I rarely felt at home.

I chose to leave everything behind: the wasted opportunities, the shiny things I had spent money on and the expectations of conventional living: the race to get a bigger house, bigger car, bigger gravestone. I would have no home, no appointments, no deadlines, no career, no beautiful possessions, no weekend hobbies, no mortgage, no bills, no commute. I would have everything I wanted.

I wanted to raise my arms and stare in wonder over waves of hazy blue mountains. I wanted to wake in my sleeping bag in the desert as the sun rose between my toes. To shiver in a frost-rimmed tent is to truly appreciate the next warm duvet. A parched desert teaches gratitude for running water. Clarion calls to be alive and to treasure life.

This is the road I decided to travel, yet another Englishman off on a journey. So there are lions and mud huts and narrow escapes and blood-red sunsets and snow-capped peaks, but really this is the story of a young person alone. Alone on a bicycle. What prompted me to write this book was the depressingly rapid realisation that I am no Superman, no chisel-jawed Victorian explorer, no larger-than-life climber of Everest. I cried a lot, I was scared a lot and I wanted to quit most of the time. If I had known at the start of the journey all that I knew by the end, there is no way I would have dared even to begin.

My plans started small but rapidly snowballed. I thought that I would like to cycle to India, but maybe then I should just keep going to Australia? And if I made it as far as Oz, then I might as well go to South America… and on it went, until I realised that I was preparing to try to cycle all the way around the planet.

At university I spent most of my time dreaming of, saving for and reading about adventure. It was only in my final year that I started to develop concrete plans. I became too busy planning my ride to do much studying, and my small bedsit filled with maps and globes. The possibilities were endless and this led to countless hours of happy, unproductive daydreaming. 'Operation HQ' was Borders bookshop on Broad Street in Oxford, a fine establishment where drinking coffee while reading books with no intention of making a purchase seemed to be actively encouraged. I would quietly fold down page corners so that I could resume my research on my next visit.

A sofa and a coffee are the finest travel companions one can have. Armchair travel is often more exciting than the real thing, and always more comfortable. The only limit is your imagination. Don Quixote said that you can 'journey all over the universe in a map, without the expense and fatigue, without the inconveniences of heat, cold, hunger and thirst'. Reading is cheaper than travelling (in paperback at least) and far more convenient. You can skip the boring parts, savour the good bits, laugh in the face of danger and drop ice cubes down the vest of fear. Sir, Madam, I applaud your choice!

This happy daydreaming could have been fine if I had kept it to myself. My travels were little more than 'dreams in the dusty recesses of my mind'. But the moment I began expanding my plans over reassuringly expensive pints of Stella Artois in the Oxford pubs, I was trapped. Make a tall claim to a friend and, no matter how successfully the beer helps him forgive and forget his own nocturnal indiscretions, he will pitilessly remind you of your boasts, until eventually there is no escape. So, word got out, and gradually the idle dream became hectic reality.

Then I was offered a job that interested me. I sat down and wrote a letter thanking them for their offer but, unfortunately, I could not accept the position because I was going to cycle round the world. Writing that letter was the moment that I realised, with a cocktail of excitement and fear in my stomach, that I was actually going to do it.

The months before departure were exciting. I attended an Expedition Planning Seminar in the hallowed rooms of the Royal Geographical Society and this gave me the confidence to take myself and my idea seriously. I absorbed book after book about great journeys and adventures and the men and women who had pulled them off. I marvelled at their accomplishments and wondered whether I could do anything remotely similar. There was only one way I would ever know.

I pored over maps and searched the internet. I spent ages trying to compile a sensible kit list. From Three Men in a Boat I learned that I must not take the things I could do with, but only the things I could not do without. That still seemed to be an awful lot of things to fit into four small panniers. Pages and pages of note pads filled with my scrawl: optimal times of the year to be in northern Australia, addresses in remote lands of unwitting friends of friends who had been offered to me as contacts, wars and monsoons to avoid, ambitious brainwaves on how to secure sponsorship, agitating lists of things that still needed to be done (Dentist! Passport photos! Bottom bracket! Money!), financial calculations on how long I could make my £7,000 of hoarded Student Loans last, insurance queries, equipment wish lists and visa information. On and on they went. I didn't really have enough money, but that was surely not a reason to not go.

I decided to ride the length of the three great landmasses on Earth: Eurasia, the Americas and Africa, joining them together to complete a circumnavigation. I would ride from my home to Australia, then from Alaska down to Patagonia and finally back home from Cape Town via West Africa and Gibraltar. I guessed it would take about three years. I thought that I would fly across the oceans. I decided to support the charity Hope and Homes for Children through my journey, raising publicity and funds for them. I cobbled together a website and began hunting for sponsorship. I couldn't believe how much needed to be done. By the time I began actually riding, I felt that the toughest stage would already be over.

I thrived on the astonishment when people heard of my plans. Never mind that I had not yet ridden a single mile: people were impressed. Friends hinted that I was being over-ambitious, that a shorter trip would be more realistic. Potential sponsors did not feel that I was a risk worth backing: why not tackle a single continent and enjoy greater odds of succeeding? One bicycle company responded with undisguised scepticism: 'Do you think we just got off the banana boat?! Of course we are not going to give you a bike for such a ridiculous idea. Go get a job if you want a bike.'

But I was determined: I wanted to make a journey that was bigger, farther and harder than anybody else could imagine. I wanted something so hard that I would surely fail unless I poured every drop of my being into it. My head was alternately up in the clouds and up my own backside.

Saying adieu to my girlfriend, was brutal. I had spent the four happiest years of my life with Sarah, but I had no interest in an office life, and Sarah was too sensible to want to cycle the world, so compromise never seemed possible for either of us. It was inevitable that a crunch time would arrive. While I scrimped and saved and planned for my journey, Sarah leaped into the racing currents of the career world and we slowly drifted apart without my realizing it. It was only when the moment of goodbye arrived that I realised how huge a part of my life she was, and just how deeply I loved her. Crying uncontrollably I tried to reassure myself that my anguish was a sign of my commitment to my journey. But that was rubbish. I was throwing away the best days of my life with my best friend for a bloody bike ride. I had never been as lonely as I watched her drive away that last time.

Foolish Preparation

How often is happiness destroyed by preparation,
foolish preparation?
Jane Austen

As I rode the peaceful, rain-sodden countryside of Germany, the atrocities of September 11th had struck. In the confused aftermath, all my plans and preparation had been swatted aside. The shockwaves and repercussions of the terrorist strikes and the outbreak of war in Afghanistan had made my planned route across Asia very dangerous.

None of this helped my state of mind which had already plumbed new depths of loneliness. Homesick, deeply upset by separation from Sarah and struck at last by the enormity of the task I had set myself, I felt overwhelmed. In those early weeks, as I tried to get my head around my new lifestyle, I had to learn how to cram everything into my panniers, how to find campsites, how to put up my new tent and use my new stove and how to choose a route away from the main roads without getting horribly lost.

I had to get fit as well. Each night my legs were wobbly, my bum was sore, and my whole body ached when I woke each morning in strange, lumpy fields across northern Europe. As I followed the Danube east I wanted nothing more than to be curled up on my sofa at home and to never do anything irresponsible again. My diary filled up with anxious, confused scrawling as

I wrestled with the new world order and its implications for my ride in a newly frightened and divided world. I swooped between moods of surrender and determination, caution and recklessness.

My passport bore visa stamps for Iran and Pakistan, all unintelligible, exotic curled calligraphy, splendid coats-of-arms and hasty signatures. In my panniers were an enormous puffy down jacket and sleeping bag to help me through a winter in the mountains of Central Asia, and in my heart were the smooth curves of the Sydney Opera House, that gleaming bay and the impossibly distant end of this road.

I looked over at the clock on the wall. My eyes took a moment to adjust, peering over the umbrella of lamplight on my table into the darkness of the sitting room. It was 3am. In just a few hours, scores of ragged cries would burst over the silent city from a forest of minarets, calling the faithful to prayer and announcing a new morning to Istanbul. My eyes stung, my belly was queasy with exhaustion. I sighed and reached out mechanically for the coffee pot. I poured the final cup, cold by now, and paused as the slow sludge of coffee grounds slid into my mug. In the morning I had to make the biggest decision since I began the ride two months ago. A lot had happened since then, and a lot was now about to change. Everything had been pointing east; east towards the sunrise that was fast-approaching as I toyed with my cold coffee.

I had been in Istanbul for a week, at the home of Caroline and Gurkan, friends of a friend, and a welcome oasis of relaxed hospitality. That morning I had been finger-painting on the balcony with their young son, Eren, staring anxiously out over the Bosporus at the far shore: Asia. I now heard Alara, their one-year-old daughter, cry briefly in the bedroom then quieten to sleep once more. The previous day we had watched in delight as she took her first ever wobbly, momentous footsteps. I drained the cold coffee and grimaced. I had distilled my future down to a rather sorry-looking list of options and I read over them for what felt like the millionth time.

POSSIBILITIES

1. Ride through Afghanistan.
   'Operation Certain Death' perhaps. But should be good for adventure.

2. Continue east to Iran/Pakistan.
   The ideal option. I have the visas and gear and have done the research. Conflict/resentments may spill over from Afghanistan. Could get to the cricket (Pakistan vs England).

3. North through Russia/the Stans.
   Still cycling eastwards. Too cold. Crazy bureaucracy. May get to the World Cup (in Japan and South Korea, Summer 2002).

4. Turn right for Africa.
   Amusing option. Sudan and Democratic Republic of Congo may cause problems. Not very sensible – equipment, visas etc. Have done no research on Africa.

5. Fly over the hotspots to India and continue from there.
   Maintains Eastward progress but the 'chain' is broken.

6. Fly to the States, do the Americas then Australia and Asia Expensive. Will probably omit Africa from the journey. Shortens overall route (a good and a bad point).

7. Just go home.

Only the final option appealed to me. I made my decision. I decided to go to bed.

Istanbul to Amman

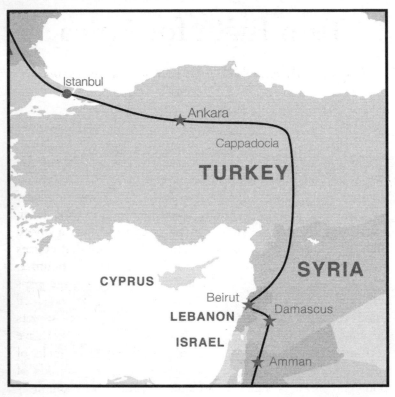

Turn Right for Africa

Cycling is like church: many attend, but few understand.
Jim Burlant

In the morning I left my bike in the house and joined the mayhem of Istanbul on foot, burrowing into the scrum, winding ever deeper and further from the tourist markets' slick multilingual sales patter, sweet at first, cloying later, nauseating by Day 2. Memories fly at me now like a photo album scattered on the floor, retaining the clarity that comes with the first exposure to a world so different from the familiar. Market stalls packed tight together, humanity filling the gaps and huge barrows of fruit or pistachio nuts being manoeuvred impossibly through it all by perspiring, shouting men; streets of shiny bath taps, streets of rugs ("Hello, my friend! I give you special price!"); streets of pirated music cassettes; sacks of spices and herbs seeping their scents; precarious pyramids of pomegranates to be squeezed into juice; old men ceremoniously sipping from glasses of amber tea, smoking apple-scented water-pipes and frowning at their backgammon boards. Sausage stalls and giant blocks of cheese and silver wet fish plucked from the Golden Horn of the Bosporus. Old sunken-eyed ladies hunched in layers of blankets, selling saucers of grain to feed frenzied squabbles of pigeons – bringers of good luck – at the entrance to the New Mosque, an Istanbul youngster at only four centuries old.

Suddenly a commotion. "Stop thief!" Cries from an open air clothes stall and a flurry in the crowd. The stall keeper yells his anger, an exposed man barges people aside and sprints away. A spontaneous lynch mob charged after the thief, men giving chase down the hill, hurdling obstacles with shopping bags flying, others sticking out impeding feet to try and trip the crook, an old woman swinging her stick. The spontaneity of the chase, unthinkable at home, was thrilling and I gave a cheer when they collared their man. The thief, hopelessly outnumbered (I did feel a twinge of British sympathy for the underdog), was roughly dragged through the jeering crowd towards the already arriving policemen. And then normality returned. I saw this thief-catching excitement three times in two days and enjoyed it thoroughly each time.

Wandering enchanted and disoriented, I grazed on snacks from street stalls, lured by scents, colours and the imploring eyes of salesmen. Sweet cups of tea, stuffed vine leaves, walnut pastries, sticky sweets and kebabs. Vendors stood on every street with slowly revolving spits of lamb and chicken. The proprietors of smoky roast chestnut stalls tried to make one final sale as they packed up for the night. The crowds flowed around them and their shouts. By the waterfront at Eminonu, rows of lamplit fish sandwich grills compete for attention, steam and smoke billowing from the bright green chillies and the grilling fish. Gentle waves splashed up the sea walls and ferries ploughed back and forth. Looking over the Bosporus towards the far shore and Asia I felt an almost magnetic pull despite my angst. Four years of dreaming and nine months of planning: preparing to cycle round the world had been intense. But things had then settled down into a simple life on the road. I had been pedalling towards Australia. I was ready for a savage winter. I was looking forward to the crowds of India. All the unique charms and frustrations of Asia awaited and I was as ready as I could be.

After September 11th though, things were more complicated. My nationality became an issue as countries were having to choose whether they were 'with us or against us' in the new 'War on Terror'. This filtered down to little me in the form of places that I could, or could not, ride through. Doors were being slammed shut all around me as nations chose sides. All my planning was useless now. I wished that I could talk it over with Sarah, but I knew that if I called her, the sound of her voice would be the final straw that would push me to quit.

Istanbul, 'the still point of the turning world', was a good place to choose a new direction, and I decided not to risk riding east to Pakistan knowing that I could be turned back at the border. I decided that only a madman would ride through Russia in winter. That left only one direction open, and Australia would have to wait, Chris and I would have to go our separate ways.

I walked out of the Syrian Consulate with a new stamp in my passport. Instead of continuing straight ahead towards Sydney, I was turning right for Africa, on my way south to Cape Town. With visas for Pakistan and Iran, clothes for a Central Asian winter, and a big map of Asia. I was not well prepared. Would I make it? Could I make it? Who would I meet? What would I see? The terrifying uncertainty of everything was intoxicating. On the way back to the house I succumbed to a kebab vendor's smiling persuasion. I walked over to a bench to eat, study my new visa and take a few deep breaths. My ride was back on track.

The kebab seller came over, a large carving knife in his hand, and gestured to ask whether he could sit down. I shuffled along the bench to make space and he sat.

"Deutsch?" he asked.

"England."

"Ah, Michael Owen!" he beamed, twisting his shoulders and wiggling his portly legs to imitate the footballer weaving his way through the opposition. The international language of football.

I laughed and took a bite of kebab, giving an appreciative "Mmm!" as I chewed. He patted his round belly approvingly and gave me a thumbs up. My enjoyment of his kebab had sealed our friendship. He stuck out his hand to shake, introducing himself as Erden. I told him I was 'Alex,' for few nationalities could manage to pronounce the brevity of 'Al' or the more unusual 'Alastair'.

"Alex... England..." he mused, hands on knees, nodding his head and looking out over the park. "Meesees Thatcher... The Beat-les... Lady Dee-aana..."

I nodded and chewed, well used to acknowledging these ambassadors for Britain.

As if suddenly remembering all that was happening in the world at that time, Erden poked my knee and turned to look at me, his face concerned beneath his fake Adidas cap.

"Bin Laden... BOOM! George Bush... BOOM!" He brandished his knife like a conductor's baton to emphasise the explosions, shaking his head with disapproval. "Afghanistan... BOOM! Tony Blair... BOOM!"

And then he laughed again.

My kebab now finished, I showed Erden the new Syrian visa in my passport. I motioned, my hands pedalling, that I was going to cycle to Syria. He found this very funny and reached to give my quads a good squeeze, checking I was up to the task. At that moment a new customer approached his stall. Erden jumped up and jogged back along the pavement, his carving knife slicing the air. Suddenly thinking of something he turned back to me and called out, "Alex! Alex! Syria... BOOM! Ha! Ha!"

Morning

A man is a success if he gets up in the morning and goes to bed
at night and in between does what he wants to do.
Bob Dylan

Mornings come peacefully on the road. I wake slowly with the daylight, turning in my sleeping bag, adjusting the bundle of clothes that act as my pillow and dozing once or twice until my head is clear and ready to begin the day. I lie still and listen to the sounds outside my tent. Sometimes birdsong, sometimes whooshing vehicles, sometimes water, sometimes silence. I unzip the tent door and feel the fresh air on my face. I check the weather and particularly the wind: strong winds can seriously spoil my day.

I climb out of the tent, barefoot, and stretch and scratch and yawn. I wander a few paces from the tent to pee, and decide if I want coffee or not. I have no idea what time it is, but I slept so early that I feel fresh even though the sun has not yet risen. I pour water from one of my bottles into my pan and light my stovehile the water heats I pack away the tent and sleeping bag, then clip my panniers back onto the bike. My packing is brisk and efficient, everything lives in its place. My movements are slick and precise. I am ready to move again. The water boils and I sit cross-legged on the ground to make coffee. I stir in a mound of sugar, and spread jam on a few pieces of bread with my spoon. While I eat I study the maps and write my diary. I pack up my stove, lick the spoon clean and shake the dregs out of the mug. I brush my teeth, pull on socks, shoes and shirt, then push the bike out onto the road from my concealed campsite. A square of crumpled grass is all I have left behind. I pull on riding mitts, reset the daily mileage total on my bike computer and pedal on my way.

I have been awake for about twenty minutes. The campsite is far behind me by the time the sun breaks above the horizon.

A new day has begun.

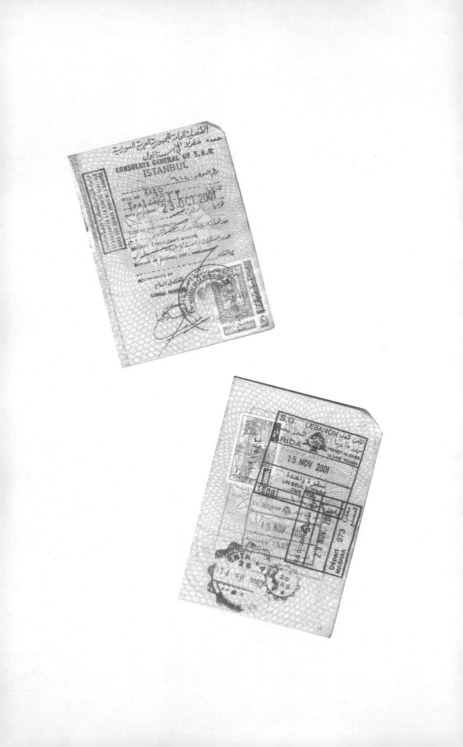

War and Terror?

The habit of persistence is the habit of victory.
Herbert Kaufman

The ride through Turkey was beautiful with varied landscapes and unstinting generosity. I climbed mountains of sharp grey flint where fragrant pine trees grew and jays and woodpeckers and hoopoes flittered. Scattered amongst the dark green pines the deciduous trees enjoyed their extravagant autumnal riot of colour. Everywhere I looked was a perfect campsite, tempting me to stop and pitch camp early. People gave me bread and cheese, yoghurt and walnuts and strangers welcomed me to stay in their homes.

I slept close to the centre of Ankara, surrounded by tower blocks and highways, but it was dark and I thought nobody would notice my tent. Four teenage boys found me. Puffing feverishly on plastic bags of solvent, they shook the tent to wake me and demanded money, alcohol, cigarettes and, tragically, the glue from my puncture kit. Wide-eyed and desperate, they frightened me. I cannot remember their faces now, only the plastic bags inflating and emptying rhythmically and their desperation. I was trying to calm them but resigned to having to fight, when out of a nearby garage a short stocky man yelled at the kids to clear off. The boys sprinted away into the night. The man suggested that I move my tent over by the garage so he could keep an eye on me while he worked the night shift. I had a lot to learn.

The rock formations at Cappadocia are one of Turkey's jewels. Accordingly they are blighted with travel agencies urging tourists to: 'Come on our tour to non-commercial, traditional villages; Camp for a night and see genuine dervish dancers'. But the scenery around Goreme was of eroded rocks and valleys, and extraordinary cave dwellings. I wandered up surreal canyons, alone in the off-season early winter, winding up and down mazes of contorted, beautifully coloured rock and growing ever more lost. Huge phalluses of eroded rock, euphemistically dubbed 'fairy chimneys', giant mushrooms, haystacks, waves, pyramids, cake icing all in whites, greys, pinks, reds and greens.

Cave dwellings and underground churches are carved out of the rock, some dating back to Biblical times. In one early church I sat by the hewn altar admiring roof paintings that had half-survived aeons of earthquakes and weathering. They felt all the more mystical for their faintness. The link between the ancient artist and the modern me was so slight and tenuous and yet, and yet, that link still was there. A chap called Baz was obviously not as impressed as I. His name was scrawled on the carving of Jesus, borne on the donkey.

At this time of year, tourists are few and the gift stall salesmen are lethargic like winter wasps. A bored onyx salesman described to me the idiosyncrasies of different nationalities. French people bought his products, Americans made a lot of noise but no action, the Japanese were too busy gazing down the alternate reality of their viewfinders, whilst the English politely said, 'No thanks' and claimed to have no money. Politely I pleaded no money, and moved on.

I rode past snowy peaks and camped near Mount Tarsus, looking back at the pink mountains in the setting sun. I camped in a field, and the farmer came to say hello and satisfy his curiosity. Ahmet was fiercely tanned and sported a fine moustache, a navy blazer and flip-flops. He shook my hand, gestured that I was welcome, and sat down in the grass to watch me set up my tent. I made tea, he enjoyed the little stove, and he politely filtered his tea leaves through his luxuriant moustache. Ahmet and I walked across a couple of fields to his home, a large open-backed trailer roofed with tight plastic sheeting. Inside was cosy, clean and simply organised; a bed, stove, food, and lamp, similar things to those I carried on the bike. He cooked sausage and eggs and we sat on the floor drinking tea together and eating, enjoying the companionship despite the lack of common language.

Nearing the Mediterranean coast I turned towards Adana and into an angry headwind. Adrian, a middle-aged English cyclist and hat collector on holiday in Turkey, had warned me, "Sorry to piss on your oil painting, mate, but there's some big bastard hills ahead!" I hit them in a beautiful sunset as I climbed out of Antakya and Hasiye. The winding road out of town was a real snoggers' paradise and I cursed all the happy couples as I pedalled past alone, wondering where I would sleep that night and what I would eat. Questions I would have to answer many hundreds of times more before I saw my own bed again. I settled to cook a pan of spaghetti and onion behind a wall in a field of heavy red soil clods. Another campsite, another full belly, another day ridden. Another snog-free day.

At dawn, I was pedalling again. A calm and grey dawn of birds singing and smoke rising straight from the chimneys of small stone homes. Farmers were just arriving in their red-brown fields, walking beside donkeys laden with bundles of firewood. Through sandstone outcrops, small orchards, slight hills and a warm sun I, curious and nervous,was about to enter the Middle East.

'We are not demanders of war and terror – but we will defend ourselves against war and terror,' shouted the banner at the border post. Ever since the British Embassy in Istanbul had 'strongly advised me' not to enter Syria I had been growing increasingly nervous. For my whole life, the Middle East had been headline news back home. Endless uncompromising images of dogmatic hatred beamed daily into my living room. In recent years, terrorist attacks by Islamic extremists worldwide had further overshadowed the vast majority of decent, genuine Muslims in the consciousness of the West. Considering myself to be a rational, open-minded, intelligent person, I was surprised now to realise how much my mind had filled subconsciously with preconceptions and prejudices about the Middle East. As war in Afghanistan escalated in retribution for the murders of September 11th, I realised that, irrationally or not, I was very scared about riding alone through the region.

I was cycling in trousers for the first time in deference to Islamic sensitivities and the annoying flapping helped remind me that all this was new. In the first village I rode through children were streaming down the road from school towards home and lunch. They looked like any school kids in the world: running and shouting or scuffing along slowly, hand-in-hand girls whispering and gossiping, boys chucking someone's bag into a tree. It was all very normal except for their school uniform: the children were dressed in green military uniforms with epaulettes of rank for the seniors. Toy soldiers and hostile welcome banners: what was this place? And, more importantly, what the hell was I doing here, an infidel on a bicycle?

The road was punctuated with billboard pictures of three men glaring down suspiciously, like Big Brother. They were the recently deceased President and his two sons. The sinister pictures showed them in a variety of roles: stern no-nonsense statesmen in suits, relaxed casual-clothed humane figures, in battle fatigues (defending against terror presumably) and chillin' out dudes in massive aviator sunglasses. As I rode into Syria I grew increasingly nervous.

The road down towards the Mediterranean coast was hilly but I hardly noticed; there was too much on my mind. I stopped for apricot jam sandwiches at the top of a long dusty hill. I knew that Muslims ate with their right hand only, but did that apply to me as well, alone on a hilltop? My left hand had jam on it: could I lick it? I had not had to worry about these matters in Turkey, with its moderate, pragmatic approach to Islam. But were things different here? And should I say I was a Christian?

Because I wasn't, but I was that more than anything else. And what about September 11th, Bush or Bin Laden? I didn't like either of them. Oh well; if I cycled really fast and put in many miles each day, I should be able to get out of this country pretty quick...

Still in this frame of mind when evening came, I needed to find somewhere to sleep. But I didn't feel comfortable camping wild, I never considered hotels and I was too scared to knock on somebody's door and ask permission to camp; but if I wouldn't camp and I was unwilling to trust anybody then I was in for a long night. I couldn't just pedal non-stop to Africa. As the sun set, I rode past an orange farm and, as a reluctant afterthought, decided to turn back to it, asking myself, like the Dr Pepper ad, 'What's the worst that can happen?' The house was run down, glass missing from window panes and warped doors that looked reluctant to either open or close. Chickens ran round the dirt yard, and apparently, the house too, for as I rounded the corner a lady wearing a headscarf was chasing two out of the door with a broom.

She stopped in surprise when she noticed meith much miming, and a nervously pounding heart, I explained myself. The lady, who I never spoke to again, smiled and gestured me inside. There was very little dialogue for much of my ride, but so much can be communicated without language.

Inside, the walls were flaking and the only furniture was an old television on a flimsy green table. On the wall was a framed swirl of Koranic calligraphy. Sitting on blankets on the floor of the sitting room and concentrating hard on the noisy television were an old man, a skinny boy of about fifteen and two men about my age, one clean shaven and one heavily bearded. Their faces were nut brown and their eyes dark and friendly. They stood to shake my hand, laughing with surprise at my arrival, sat me down and made me welcome. Nipping outside to see my bike, they sent the lady off to make tea.

So far, so good, I thought. Maybe they won't kill me just yet. A low round table was rolled out and covered with newspaper. We all sat around it (except for the wife who ate somewhere else) and ate from communal bowls at very high speed. Soup, chicken, yoghurt, salad, bread and spinach quickly disappeared. They still hadn't killed me after we had all devoured several communal plates of food, with a very un-British haste. (Mental note: seems as though eating is with the right hand but don't worry too much about tearing bread etc with both hands.) Then the old man crushed me at chess and I tried in vain to claim a long day's ride as an excuse. I learned a few words of Arabic and I explained my trip with charades, drawings and maps, making another mental note to get an explanatory letter about my journey translated into Arabic as soon as I could. The family sought my opinion on what I thought I should feed their stupidly grinning guard dog to make him a bit tougher and a little less friendly. One of the men looked a bit like Osama bin Laden, and he began doing a comical impression of him, bouncing around the room shooting imaginary Brits and Americans. We all laughed together. Their opinion of the September 11th attacks seemed to be that, while the arrogance of America definitely needed addressing, this had been an evil way of making a statement.

We watched the news on TV, a fuzz of dreadful filming, droning monologues and lots of propaganda. When a clip of the late President was shown the family seemed genuinely upset. But still they did not kill me, and I soon learned that Syria is by no means a 'dry' country as we polished off a bottle of Arak, anise-flavoured and strong, toasting what for all of us had been a very random, unexpected, but entertaining evening. I slept that night alongside the other young men on a pile of woolly blankets on the floor. They settled themselves into comfortable positions with little grunts and coughs after locking the door and turning off the light. Outside, fields of orange trees surrounded the house and the guard dog chased chickens and wagged his tail. In the morning my new friends waved me off with a gift of a huge bag of oranges. The horrors of the Middle East? Maybe this wouldn't be so bad after all.

Much more relaxed, I rode past laden orchards and wiry olive groves on to the Lebanon border at Lattakya. One of the armed border guards was very fat, and I joked with the guards that when I began cycling, I too had been that large. They all found this hilarious. Except fat boy. He was not amused. So I left before he could get his hands on my passport. Away from the border I lay back on a warm verge of long grass and looked around. To my right was the blue sea, and to my left were snowy mountains. The call to prayer carried up to me from a nearby village.

In a small village, I stopped to ask for water at the smartest house, the only two-storey building, which had ornate metal gates. There was no fence, but the gates were nice. I walked round the locked gates and knocked on the door. I was invited inside by a stern-looking man. I got a shock when he took off his red and white *kiffiyeh*. I wasn't expecting a skinhead-with-quiff hairstyle. His wife had gold teeth and small blue facial tattoos. I helped their young daughter with her English homework whilst her Dad roasted coffee beans in a pan with a handle about a metre long. I smiled at them over my coffee cup, refilled my bottles with thanks and rode on.

As dusk settled, a massive hill appeared. So too did a very slow cement lorry, and as it passed me I dashed after it and grabbed hold, panting, for a smoky tow up the hill. Weary after a 95-mile ride, and emboldened after yesterday's kindness, I knocked on the first door I saw at the top, which turned out to be an old people's home, to ask permission to camp. The door was answered by Monsieur Tignet. Although he was aged about 80 he seemed to be running the home rather than staying in it. He waved me inside without hesitation, and he offered me a bed for the night.

Monsieur Tignet was a hunched, slow, cheerful soul. Originally from Toulouse, he had lived in Lebanon for the past 25 years. His eyebrows reached for the stars in jubilant bushiness. His mind was faster than his shuffling slippered feet. His damp eyes shone, and I wondered if the spectacles that dangled round his neck might not have been better employed perched on the end of his nose. We drank strong coffee and he reminisced about his own bike rides, proud to have once climbed Switzerland's famous St. Bernard Pass. He was miles away from me now, a young man touring the sun-drenched France and Switzerland of his mind, panniers packed with bread, salami and fruit picked from the trees. This became a common feature on my ride. So many people I met had some sort of cycling experience to share with me. All would begin modestly, "It's nothing like yours, but I went on a bike trip once…" And then they would be off, vivid memories flowing off the tongue as they recalled adventures and mishaps, enormous appetites and favourite campsites, examples of hospitality and huge hills conquered. They were all wrong though: their trips were like mine. Our memories were the same, our lives had been enriched in the same way by the purity and freedom of a long bike ride. I never met anybody who regretted doing a ride. But I met many who regretted not having done one.

My French coped, more or less, with Monsieur Tignet's long tales, but my glass of red wine was hauling down my eyelids, hammering my brain to sleep after the long day's ride. Monsieur Tignet was bursting with stories, though. I could not let my tiredness stop him from enjoying a ride that he would never ride for real again. He had been very vague and swerved away from the subject, but I gathered that his departure from France had been swift, and a return unlikely.

The next day, I zipped along the squalid seashore towards the skyscrapers and noise of Beirut. The road was lined with grotty tower blocks, neglected for many years. The traffic became quite fun once I immersed myself in the madness, combining recklessness and angry gesticulations with apologetic shrugs and appeasing smiles. There were tented shanty camps of refugee Palestinians lining the roads, and many Syrians looking for work. One sagging tarpaulin household on the roadside had wooden crates outside for seats. The family watched the roaring traffic from beneath the shade of a Haagen-Dazs parasol on this 'veranda'. Amongst the noise and fumes on the central reservation of the motorway, a barefoot boy in dirty, baggy trousers and a black and white *kiffiyeh* tended his grubby sheep, unperturbed by the 21st century, frantic all around him.

Beirut sprawled for miles, but its hub was squashed tight between the sea and the mountains. Burger King, McDonald's, Pizza Hut, neon signs in English and French, Mercedes and BMW: the trappings of a big city all piled on top of each other. I asked directions from policemen on Harley Davidsons, who helped to point me gradually closer to the street I was searching for.

I had first been invited to give a talk at the International School in Istanbul, and afterwards the Principal suggested that I contact similar schools along my route. I emailed schools in the next few countries, and some were bold enough to invite me. Thus, a wandering, unemployed stranger came into their expensive schools to tell their pupils stories of determined career avoidance. Fortunately it is easy to entertain children with tales of eating bizarre animals, sleeping in absurd locations and forfeiting showers for week upon week so my slideshows were enjoyed, and references followed. These talks raised some money for *Hope and Homes for Children* as well as helping me find places to stay and new friends in cities around the world. By the end of my journey I had given approximately 300 slideshows to many thousands of children.

One person who emailed and invited me to their school was Raymond, a teacher who also invited me to stay in his apartment, high on one of Beirut's hills. Raymond was from Sierra Leone, and he had Lebanese parents. Forced to abandon his successful beach restaurant in Sierra Leone and flee the country overnight when anarchy erupted, he had spent the last five years teaching physics in Beirut.

Knocking on his door I was greeted by loud Vivaldi and a smell of strong coffee. Raymond greeted me warmly, and I accompanied him to the Lebanese American University to see a production of Macbeth. Tonight, the Scottish play in Beirut. Roquefort and red wine last night. This ride was getting surreal. Like the rest of Beirut, the theatre was full of beautiful girls. My life felt so much simpler when I was out on the road and able to forget about women for a while.

The play began, to much whooping and cheering from the audience, and I turned my attention to the stage. Even when the actors began to speak the noise levels didn't drop much and two men had to walk up and down the aisles shushing everyone. For the first few minutes I thought that the play was in Arabic. "Nice twist," I thought. But then I caught an English word and gradually realised that the play was actually in English after all, but that the actors could not pronounce a single word. The play was a contemporary interpretation and all the players looked like neo-Nazis. Except for Macbeth: he had a horrible ponytail. Lady Macbeth could act a bit but everyone else was awful. The show degenerated into high farce. The audience became a crowd. Every entrance and exit was greeted with a riot of applause. The poor players strutted and fretted their hour upon the stage, and Macbeth delivered his lines louder and louder, faster and faster, in a permanent, hunched-over, agonised rage. Come the emotional 'tomorrow and tomorrow' soliloquy (delivered at top speed, top volume and flat on his back, looking up at the roof) I was crying with laughter to the last syllable, kneeling on the floor and holding my stomach. The cast received a roaring standing ovation at the end. I woke the next morning with sore stomach muscles from too much laughing. In my mind, Macbeth will be forever entwined with Beirut.

I went with Raymond to eat at the home of some people he knew from Sierra Leone. I sat next to 20-year-old Ronald who had just spent a year in prison. As Jehovah's Witnesses, they would not bear arms. He had refused to do National Service duty and so had been sent to jail. I admired his conviction. Every time his mother bustled past the table bearing plates of food she would fondly ruffle his hair. They were nice people and the food was great, so I stuffed a bread roll in each ear to dampen the preaching and enjoyed the fabulous mix of Lebanese and spicy West African cooking.

I bade farewell to Raymond, and went to stay with an American couple, Art and Sandy. Art was the Principal of the

American International College in Beirut, and had invited me to give a talk to his school. Art had pedalled across the USA when he was fifty, so he understood my ride. He has promised himself he will do it again, into the headwind next time, when he is sixty. He urged me to break it down into manageable chunks and targets, rather than quivering in the shadow of the vast entirety. If I did that, then the whole absurd project could begin to look more feasible: get to Cairo, into Sudan, out of Sudan, into Kenya, Cape Town. Little by little, slowly, slowly....

Shops were selling Christmas paraphernalia for Lebanon's sizeable Christian community. One had novelty Bin Laden masks alongside the Santa hats. I went to the legendary Pepé's restaurant beside the small harbour in Biblos, the oldest continuously inhabited town on Earth. Before the war, Pepé's was one of *the* places to be seen at in the Mediterranean and the walls were lined with hundreds of photos of film stars and glamorous people who had eaten there: Marlon Brando, Brigitte Bardot. As their menu claims, 'Lebanon without Pepé's' is like spending your honeymoon with a eunuch.'

At the American School I met Aimee, a Lebanese teacher. She told me her memories of the war, of her windows being sandbagged and playing cards for hours in the basement bomb shelter. For a whole year she did not go to school. She was grateful now to have been too young to register all the terror. The whole city was ravaged by seventeen years of civil war but this is nothing new for Beirut, described by Nadia Tueni as 'one thousand times dead and one thousand times born again'. Beirut had now been renovated in style once again. After the war there was a compulsory sale of property in the city centre so that the renovation project would not be hampered by any unsightly little corner shops. The streets were now wide, spotless and gleaming. Streetlights bathed the pedestrian areas in warm, safe light. Bored soldiers ambled, their rifles swinging like handbags, looking like all the other strollers. It was a beautiful city, full of hope for a peaceful, prosperous future.

Aimee and I walked together along the Corniche, a pedestrian strip along the seashore popular with joggers and middle-aged power walkers wearing sun visors, jewellery and full make-up. A jogger passed dressed in baggy Arabic dress with his anorak hood up and brogues on his feet. An old man fishing with a simple cane plucked two fish from the sea. His hi-tech rivals pretended not to notice. It was a welcome respite to laugh away a lazy weekend with an attractive woman. The knowledge that I could be doing that every weekend if I had stayed at home wrestled in my head with all the precious memories and experiences I had relished so far on the road. The warm, low sun shone on the mountains, the mountains that I would have to cross to get to Damascus. I pushed away thoughts of riding, of the vast distance that lay ahead of me, and the futility of continuing at all given my certain conviction that I would not be able to finish what I had begun.

The month of Ramadan began with festivities and a holiday mood. For a lunar month Muslims would not, or should not, eat or drink between dawn and dusk. I feared being very hungry for a month, but infidels as well as those on a journey are not expected to participate so I was well exempted. The reality of modern Ramadan is that food consumption actually increases during the month. 'Try now the new Ramadan specials!' suggested the posters in Dunkin' Donuts for the enormous fast-breaking feasts, known as *iftars*, that every family enjoys together at sunset. Later, mosques are packed for the evening prayers and a worshipful overflow crowds the pavements. A soft rumble, like waves on a gravel shore, rolls round as thousands kneel and stand as one, united in prayer, or *salah*. It is a wonderful season to be in a Muslim country.

Throughout Ramadan I made an effort to be off the roads before sunset. Cycling around that time was foolhardy as every Muslim was driving home half-crazed with hunger and *nothing* was going to get in his way. The sociable generosity of the Middle East that I was fast discovering seemed even greater during Ramadan and people were even more eager to welcome me into their homes to share their *iftar*. I had quickly come to trust, respect and like the people in the Middle East and my prejudices and fears had evaporated. At *iftar* families sit expectantly around laden tables waiting Pavlov-like for the signal from the local mosque that is the official adjudicator of the time of sunset. The signal given, the feast begins! And what a feast. There are starters that would easily make a meal in themselves: salads, olives, *houmous, baba ghannouche,* soft bread, crispy bread, vine leaves stuffed with rice, *tabouleh,* cream cheese, dates, lentil soup, apricot juice. And then come the main courses – *kebbeh,* chicken stew and more. Sickly pastries, tea and coffee would completely finish me off without a doubt the greatest eating of my journey so far was at those *iftars.*

On the 27th November 2001, I was a quarter of a century old. More than a third of my allotted lifespan gone, and there I was sat on my arse in Beirut too scared to ride on towards Africa and too scared to go home. I spent the day feeling uneasy about how much I wanted to do in life and how little time was left. Twenty-five. Twenty-five. Twenty-five. Twenty-five! However I said it, I didn't like it. I explained to Art and Sandy how much I feared getting ready to hit the road again, how nervous and upset I became each time I severed my fragile new roots. Sandy played me a song called 'Pre-Road Downs,' and reassured me that I was not alone. In the evening I went with Art down to the local ping-pong club and lost badly. It was time to ride again.

Navigating out of Beirut was difficult. "Is this the way to Damascus?" I kept asking people.

"Damascus is in Syria, this is Lebanon. It is too far to cycle. The mountains are too big. It is not possible for you," came the replies.

"Just tell me the damn way," I wanted to snap back. Throughout the world my requests for directions were hampered by people telling me that the nearby place in question was too far to cycle to.

The road climbed for hours, up above the fumes of Beirut, past a peace memorial of a tower of military tanks embedded in concrete, high above the sea into the rocky mountains towards the ski slopes and famous cedar trees. There were many soldiers on the road and at every roadblock the officers used their authority to stop me and ask me what I was doing simply to satisfy their curiosity. Posters of the weasels from Syria abounded; the presence of Syria was never far away in Lebanon, especially in these wild heights.

In the town of Baalbek I put my tent up alongside some of the most spectacular Roman temples on Earth. It was a stunning campsite. I read that they were 'temples where blood sacrifices, wine orgies and free love were means of experiencing oneness with the Gods'. It sounded a lot better than my Sunday school. The temple of Bacchus was the best preserved: from the outside it looked brand new. The temple of Jupiter is vast, greater even than anything built in Rome. Close by is Hajar-al-Habla, the largest building block in the world. Weighing 1,200 tonnes, 24 times more than those of Stonehenge, 40,000 men were needed to shift it. The Romans had intended to build the momma of all temples using this size of brick. Sadly it was only moved a short distance before somebody with some common-sense put a stop to the silliness. It is an unbelievable example of ambition, optimism and biting off more than you can chew. But, if you don't try you'll never know. Today the brick lies wonky and unused in an old quarry. There is a superstition that touching it aids fertility. The prospect of years sitting on a hard bicycle saddle prompted me to go and give it a big hug.

The temple of Bacchus was etched with old graffiti such as 'PJ Tawil et fils 1882'. I was just the latest in the long chain of hundreds of years of worshippers, travellers and gawpers on my way through the Fertile Crescent. The sun was setting and the day was turning to cold evening. I sat on a fallen column to write my diary. The vast stone columns turned a soft apricot shade in the sunset while the dirty town below was air-brushed away by winter mist. The mountains around were covered in clean snow. The red sun had set. The sky was pale lilac and the colour seeped now from the temples leaving black silhouettes against the sky. My peace was accentuated by the far-off cries from the mosques as the town settled down to break their fast. I felt like the only person left in the world. Solitude. I was once again at peace with myself and with my ride. I had no inkling of how fast that would all change.

My jubilant mood was dampened however when I climbed into my tent and realised that I had stupidly left my sleeping mat and sleeping bag back down in Beirut. I cursed myself and the thought of the freezing night ahead. I remembered now that when I packed my bags to leave Beirut I had been pleased with how compact everything had looked. I must have left the sleeping bag in the basement of Art and Sandy's house where it had been hanging to air. I put on every scrap of clothing I had, put my feet inside one pannier, my head in another and lay down on top of the other two on the cold tent floor to wait for morning. I could have moved to a nearby £1 hotel but that never occurred to me as an option, so fiercely was I budgeting. As a consolation treat I allowed myself the final two squares of a bar of chocolate that I had hoarded since Belgrade. I was frozen and tired by morning. I used a section of Roman column as a breakfast table, brewing up welcome cups of coffee and feeling the warmth ooze back into my bones.

I certainly did not fancy another cold night but I could not return to Beirut as my visa was fast expiring. So I decided to push on forwards instead. I crossed the border back to Syria and after a very hard, fast ride, arrived in Damascus. I was supposed to be staying with Fari, a friend of someone I had met in Beirut. The prospect of being able to stay with a nice family was even sweeter than usual. I asked a teenager on the street for directions and he offered to phone Fari's house for me. Unfortunately she was not yet home so Tarek invited me to his own house for *iftar*. Throughout the meal Tarek's father told me of the 'Satanic evil' of the Western press. He explained that the Holocaust did not actually happen and revealed to me that the September 11th attacks (and everything else it seemed, including Waterloo and the French and Russian Revolutions) were the fault of the Jews. After the pleasant food and unpleasant rantings I rode deep into Damascus in the dark towards Fari's house. I asked for directions at a florist's and the man there kindly phoned Fari for me. She told him that she was going out later on so it was not convenient for me to go round to her house. My weariness amazed me, I was branded on my feet and now I had no one to meet. It was late but the florist helped me, patiently writing directions in Arabic to the cheapest migrant workers' hostel that he knew.

And so I rode several miles back the way I came.

I had ridden a long way that day, I had not slept much the night before. And now I was riding through the potholed, dark streets of a strange city with no idea where I was going, since I could not read the Arabic directions on my scrap of paper. All I could do was stop at every junction, show the directions to somebody and follow the direction of their pointing arm.

An hour later I made it to the hostel, shattered and scared. It was a complete dump. At least it was cheap and safe. It had been a long, long day. The price was clearly signed as £2, but for me it was £3. I began to protest but I then felt hot tears welling. I meekly handed over my money and locked myself and my bike in the room at the end of a dark corridor, next to the stinking, flooded, communal toilet.

I flopped onto the brown itchy blanket on the creaking wire bed and crumpled into tears and, eventually, into exhausted sleep.

Self-Chosen Pain

Even as the stone of the fruit must break,
that its heart may stand in the sun,
So must you know pain…
Much of your pain is self-chosen.
Khalil Gibran

I was warm, I was safe and I had nothing to do all day. It was mid-morning and I was still in bed. It should have been a relaxing, lazy rest, but, as I lay in bed, I found myself sliding slowly into tears once again. Beginning with a frown, then brimming eyes, a fat rolling tear and finally full flowing crying. For the whole day in that windowless, filthy room, I cried my eyes out. Every move I made was slow and deliberate for fear of breaking up completely. It was not just crying; it was gut wrenching, shoulder heaving, uncontrollable sobbing. My whole body ached. It was the surfacing, like an angry pus-filled boil, of a festering subconscious knowledge that I had been denying for a long time.

I was not going to make it round the world. I could not stick it out. I had bitten off more than I could chew. It was too hard. I was not up to it. I was going to fail. It was my dream life and I didn't want it.

I had been riding for three months and it felt like a hell of a long time. Thousands of miles of sweat and lactic acid; hauling myself and my gear across fourteen countries. I could not believe how far I had pedalled, and yet the map made a mockery of my efforts. England to Damascus was a laughable fraction of what I had set out to do. I had so far to go. I was no way near. I had no chance. Sooner or later, I realised, I was going to fail.

What was most likely to end my resistance was not hardship, or one horrific experience, but the wild bucking of emotions. I had seen beautiful places and met great people, but I had also been afraid and lonely and exhausted. During those days in Damascus, I was absolutely on the brink of riding out to the airport to jack it all in and return home. I have never been so low in my life. It was the closest I ever came to surrendering. As Graham Greene said: 'Despair is the price one pays for setting oneself an impossible aim.'

Steadily but relentlessly since I left home, the peaks and troughs of my emotions had been growing ever greater, and the time between them decreasing. The suddenness with which I crashed or bounced was alarming. It was so different from my home life, where waves of emotion had rippled like the wake of a canal boat. Nowadays they leaped up and crashed down, higher and higher, lower and lower. Delirious highs howling with joy at the sky, and then numbing lows of forsaken desolation on empty, endless roads. I didn't know how to cope with this, I had not prepared for it. Faster and faster they came, like a cartoon machine, whirring and smoking, racing and flashing and beeping, quicker and louder, higher and lower, towards an inevitable conclusion: the spectacular explosion. This see-sawing could not go on much longer.

The cycling was nothing. That was easy once the muscles tightened to their tasks. It was the mind games that were breaking me. At the centre of them was Sarah. I was aware that I could be using her as a focus for my insecurities and anxieties. I still felt that if I had never met Sarah then I would be having a ball now. But, as the old song goes, 'I have kissed you, so I'll miss you.' My life on the road had all that I had yearned for back home: risk, adventure, uncertainty, challenge and variety. But in return for devil-may-care freedom

I had bartered security, friendship, human contact, familiarity, and love. Signing the pact made me understand what I had given up.

I had so many pictures of Sarah in my mind, haloed by memory, of times of pure happiness. Her delight and excitement opening presents; her brow frowning in concentration at her desk; wrapped up warm in my scarf on Castle Hill in Edinburgh, her nose cold and her cheeks and eyes glowing... And here I was lying on my own in a poop-hole Syrian dormitory and Sarah was at home eating takeaway alone in front of the TV.

What the hell had I done? Yet I had chosen to leave Sarah. Surely the ride was as important to me as she was. That was a startling realisation.

Missing Sarah was partly my being scared by the prospect of Africa. Sudan was gnawing at my subconscious: visas, war, deserts. The poverty of Ethiopia, the crime-ridden Kenyan capital were far beyond my realm of experience.

I asked myself over and over how I had the audacity and arrogance to think that I could pedal through Africa. How could I have committed myself to years of this madness, of being the odd one out, of knowing no-one or nowhere?

I was torn: if I succeeded it would be a big achievement. I would see and do fantastic things. I thought that I would be genuinely happy and satisfied. Certainly my life would be enriched. If I quit and went home, I would have Sarah. At the time I was too self-absorbed to reflect in terms of what would be the best for both of us. It was all just about me, me, me.

I had tried my best, but it had just been too difficult. Only my pride was unable to accept that I had failed. Only conceit forbade me to fly home. To escape was so easy, the modern traveller's shameful secret − a quick ride to the airport, crack out the Visa card and that would be it. Back home in time for tea. But, despite how upset I had repeatedly been, despite how easy escape would have been, despite it all, I did not go to the airport. Surely this meant that I did want to be there. I wanted to scream with frustration.

I felt trapped on an endless rollercoaster.

I tried to focus on why I wanted to continue, hoping to highlight the positives. I had always felt that if I found something better to do with my life than riding around the world then I would do it. I had not begun the ride solely with the purpose of reaching the end. But I had not thought of, and still haven't, anything more exciting and rewarding. I knew that if I quit that I was likely to regret it one day. I thought of how frustrating life had been in England, and how eager I had been to get away from comfort and complacency. I thought of all the experiences I would miss by going home. I was lucky. The stars had aligned, the combination locks had clicked crisply into place, the roulette ball had danced and bounced and fallen right. I had an ambition, and I had the opportunity to pursue it. It was now or never for my dream of many years. Was I going to give that up? I appreciated the words of Charlotte Bronte who wrote: 'It is a very strange sensation to inexperienced youth to feel itself quite alone in the world. The charm of adventure sweetens that sensation, the glow of pride warms it: but then the throb of fear disturbs it.'

I needed to learn to be less uptight, less consumed by money, less bedevilled by how many miles I covered each day, and less obsessed with reaching my next sanctuary. I was going to cycle through Africa. I would encounter beauty and I would meet good people. If I was weary: rest. If I was afraid: leave. If night was falling: sleep. If I was hungry: eat. I did not need to make it harder on myself by a constant refusal to take the easy option. Searching for yourself you will always find demons. I was trying to be a free man, grasping for talismans. Right then I was not sick, scared or in danger. I was in a hotel, my bike still worked and I still had money. What would I be like when things became tough? I needed to get positive. The Sufi poet Hafiz wrote: 'Though the way is full of perils, and the goal far out of sight, there is no road to which there is no end: do not despair.'

My diary that night: '*Lessons learned today: Don't make big decisions when tired, lonely, hungry, frightened, ill or at night.*'

Next day I rode slowly into Damascus and explored the *souk*, the market. It was Friday, the Syrian day off, so the *souk* was quiet and calm, just what I needed. The empty ancient streets were too dead for dreaming, too dark and gloomy. The balconies of the first floor crookedly overhung the streets, almost touching each other. Aromatic spices filled the air. I wandered slowly and aimlessly, feeling fragile. A tiny, waist-high arched door led into the peaceful courtyard of a black-and-white striped mosque. I took off my flip-flops and the marble floor was cool on my bare feet as I soaked in the serenity.

Back in the market some stalls worked by candlelight, others were highlighted in a shaft of sunlight or plugged in to dodgy overhead wires. A black tin roof meant there was little light in the winding *souk*, but in parts where the roof was tatty with tiny rust-eaten holes, dots of sunlight shafted through. On one street the ceiling was peppered with used tea bags hurled up against the roof where they had stuck. The string and paper tabs from the tea bags trembled with the breeze. They reminded me of school where a solitary strand of spaghetti had dangled undisturbed from the canteen ceiling for years.

Merchants sat and presented their wares, haggled with customers or sipped steaming glasses of tea. I picked out some dried apricots and wondered how the man would be able to leave his cubicle to serve me. He seemed trapped for eternity behind his ancient sacks of wrinkly fruit. Above his head was a length of rope and, like Tarzan in a turban, he swung out onto the pavement, grinning at my surprise. The confusing spider's web of narrow streets still reflected the old Roman plans.

Straight Street runs from a high-arched ancient city gate right through the heart of the *souk*. It is mentioned in the Bible in the story of Paul: 'And the Lord said to Ananias: "Get up and go to the street called Straight, and at the house of Judas look for a man of Tarsus named Saul."' Today, amid the gentle hum of traders, little felt to have changed. Much though had changed in the spiritual lives of the Damascans in that time. This is best reflected by the Great Umayyad Mosque which has served time as a temple, a church and a mosque. I sat quietly outside the mosque, one of my favourites, and one of Islam's earliest, dating from when the religion first sprang from the Arabian peninsula. An old man with a long white beard read his Koran beside me. A quiet group of women waited outside the mosque, draped from head to toe in black. Only their eyes showed, huge, deep brown and kohl framed, firing my imagination into all sorts of inappropriate, un-Koranic scenarios. Men stood around talking, separate from the women, colourful in their red and white *kiffiyehs*. They shouted at each other, smoked, and did a lot of hacking and spitting. I wondered if it was time to start purifying my water. The call to prayer sang out and the faithful shuffled into the courtyard, to wash their feet at the long rows of taps before entering the mosque to pray. Alone, I drank in the stillness of a devout Muslim city during the Friday lunchtime prayers.

Fari phoned the hostel and invited me for *iftar*. She was American-Syrian and her husband Saadalla was Syrian. They were affluent and well-groomed, clearly did not often encounter scruffbags like me, and did not look as though they intended to make it a habit. It was very kind of Fari to invite me, as she was not in the least bit interested in me and hurried to switch on the TV as soon as her maids appeared to clear the dinner plates. I remember the news that day for they announced the death of the Beatle, George Harrison. Saadalla was nice, well educated and charming, but he too believed that September 11th was the work of the FBI or the Israelis. Everyone I met in Damascus seemed to think this and scoffed at my doubts. In turn I worried at the indoctrinated, unquestioning mindset of many Muslims.

The food was delicious and, as usual at *iftar*, more than we could ever eat. Their son wasn't hungry though as his friend had just brought him back a Big Mac all the way from Beirut. (Things like McDonald's, Coca-Cola and ATM's do not exist in Syria.) His verdict was: 'Cold but delicious!'

After dinner, Saadalla helped me solve the case of the missing sleeping bag. Some big mountains, about 200 kilometres and an international border stood between me and my sleep.

We emailed Art and Sandy and asked them to send the sleeping bag in a taxi. It sounded like a very dodgy plan but Saadalla saw no problem with it: '*Inshallah*, God willing, no problem.' I had to trust his judgement. I left their plush apartment and massive telly and cycled back through the rain to the stinking hostel to twiddle my thumbs.

I rode back to their house the next evening, and my sleeping bag had actually arrived. Rain fell in floods, and waves rose from beneath cars and crashed their tons on me cartoon style, but I was relieved and grateful to Fari and Saadalla that I had a sleeping bag once more.

One of the appeals of bike travel is that you arrive gradually. None of the shock of rolling a trolley out of an air-conditioned airport and into the sudden sweating chaos of the developing world. The heat! The noise! The smell! The crowding clamour of men eager to carry your bags, to find you a taxi, to find you a hotel, and to con you while you are still soft and *naïve*. By bike you experience the proximity or distance between people and places. That forms some of the ways they interact, or do not interact, and consequently how the very history of our planet has unfurled. You appreciate the world as a single, gradually morphing blend rather than the separate, isolated communities that air travel and television suggest. This was very apparent in Damascus. I kept forgetting that this is one of the most ancient cities on earth. The spice markets and hooting taxis, bushy moustaches and kebab stalls, historic heaving streets and noisy mosque loudspeakers all seemed quite normal. It showed how ideal faithful Rita was for slipping me gradually from one environment to the next, allowing me to experience the world as a single entity.

I returned to the *souk* in the old town. It was a new morning, the rain had stopped, the sun was out and I was damn well going to cheer up. I changed some dollars through a melodramatic hushed negotiation with an old man in his grocery store. I bought some provisions, and dragged myself out of my torpor. My worrying about how little money I had stopped when I blew a little bit of it. Saving my Student Loans, I had accrued a total fortune of £7,000. It was going to be tough to make that last the duration of the ride, but it was all that I had so it had to last. Two tasty kebabs inside me, and I felt considerably happier.

I liked a painting of the *souk* in an art shop, but wondered why the artist had included all the ugly telephone wires. A romanticised painting that I saw later of the *souk* complete with camels showed me why. We need not be ashamed of travelling in a modern era, and part of the charm of Damascus today is the blend of the old and the new, so why not show the seriously dangerous wiring in your paintings?

Next day I woke up happy, solid in the acceptance that I may not manage to finish the journey. I had worked through my frightening mental collapse, thought hard about its causes, effect and remedies, and gained a better idea of my capabilities, my limits, and my motivations. I would just do my best and when I had had enough, I would try to accept it. I would try to do what I felt was right, and not what I thought other people would want me to do. I packed up the panniers for the bike, and began to potter slowly through Syria towards Jordan. I did a lot of thinking even though I kept trying not to. I was trying to be positive as I rode, to think of just one day at a time. I sang, very loudly, to get my mojo back.

I camped in a newly ploughed field on earth the colour of a chocolate cake. The bright pink clouds paled to silver as the sun sank. The mosque nearby, there was always a mosque nearby, signalled sunset and *iftar* began. The roads were empty, and bellies were being filled. I was happy to be alone. In the fading light I sat outside my tent and read Christina Rossetti:

Better by far you should forget and smile,
Than that you should remember and be sad.

Camping

There lives and there leaps in me
A love of the lowly things of earth,
And a passion to be free.
To pitch my tent with no prosy plan,
To range and to change at will,
To mock at the mastership of man,
To seek Adventure's thrill,
Carefree to be, as a bird that sings,
To go my own sweet way.
Robert Service

Whenever I told people that I slept rough, they were horrified by the dangers. Wild animals, psychopaths, lumpy ground, and a lack of showers and toilets all come up as reasons to book into a hotel. Even people happy to camp wild at home baulk at the thought of it in far-flung lands. Whenever I ride with new companions, I see their hesitation in choosing a shelter for the night. Perhaps there is some vestige of animal instinct that urges caution when we are asleep and defenceless. Perhaps our imaginations conjure spectres of monsters and murderers. The first time I camped alone, behind a hedge in a muddy field near Calais, I read The Times, ate a Pot Noodle and jumped at the slightest gust of wind or cracking twig. But familiarity had bred contentment, and I began mastering the arts of wild camping. I came to love sleeping rough and free, and I never tired of it, though it was often hard work and stressful.

Sometimes I miss the simplicity of turning a key in a lock and opening the door to a safe home, warm and dry, with a shower, a table and chair, a light to read by, a fridge full of food, running water, and a comfortable bed waiting. Every time I camp it is in a place I have never been before. I have to search for a site and set up the camp. Every day there is an element of risk. Should I stop early to savour a beautiful campsite, or squeeze out as many miles as possible? If I am close to a town, should I hold steady for the night before I reach it, or push on past it before stopping? Is the town small enough to pass before darkness? Are there likely to be safe hiding spots on the other side, or should I take what I can find now? Do I have chores to do in the town in the morning, or do I want to get past it and maximise tomorrow's distance, unhindered by negotiating a new city? Is this area safe enough to camp wherever I feel like, or must I hide, or even wait for the cover of darkness before camping? How remote is the land? Will I be discovered here? Do I need to hide under a bridge or in a forest? Should I ask permission to camp? It's always safer and more interesting, but do I have the energy tonight to explain my life to strangers yet again? Do I have the strength to ride fast until darkness or would I rather loaf early with a book, popcorn and a cup of tea? Do I have enough food and water to stop for the night?

I set myself daily targets, choosing a time, a distance or a hilltop that has to be gained before I allow myself to begin scouting for a campsite. I am an expert now at seeking out a place to sleep, weighing up the variables in split seconds as I ride along, knowing that a comfortable, safe, undetected sleep depends on a good decision. I look for places out of sight of people and buildings and the road, and away from dogs that pick up my scent and bark all night. I look for good cover: hills, dead ground, trees, hedges or walls. I look for flat land, grassy or sandy and free of thorns. Running water is an irresistible luxury for the chance to swim and wash. I look for paths or tracks that lead away from the road and noisy traffic. Some nights are paradise. Others are no more than a safe place to lay my head for a few hours like a fugitive. Between the rows in a cornfield, a steep hillside, a ditch, under a motorway bridge, a rubbish dump, a drainage pipe, a central reservation and an abandoned building all offer refuge.

Upon spotting a potential campsite I have to decide in a moment whether to brake and check it out, or to continue in the hope of finding something better. If I stop, I leave the bike and walk to check out the site. If it is OK, I then wait for there to be no vehicles passing, so that I am completely unseen. Then I wheel the bike from the road and into my hide-out. Finally I lie down and relax.

Another day is done.

Hues of Youth

Only those who will risk going too far can possibly find out
how far one can go.
TS Eliot

Approaching the Jordanian border I tried to spend my final Syrian coins. I ate at a pancake stall with an appetizing view of a butcher hanging a camel's bloody head and neck on a hook. The pancake seller, smiling, refused my money, as did the man I tried to buy a block of dates in treacle from. The man I bought a cake from would not take my money either. In the end I gave up and changed my Syrian pounds for Jordanian dinar in a hardware shop. I thought back to the British Embassy in Istanbul warning me of the perils of Syria. I reflected on the perils of preconceptions.

As I left Syria the border guards were watching the TV show, *Home and Away*. In no-man's land, three men with rifles blocked the road and would not let me continue. I had no idea what they wanted. They argued amongst themselves for a few minutes before walking away up the road. I shrugged and pedalled on into Jordan.

I waited 10 days in Amman for two friends, Simon and Arno, to arrive. We were at Oxford together, and they came to join me for a Christmas bike ride. I used my time in the tricky task of securing a Sudanese visa. Travelling overland to South Africa involves crossing Sudan, Angola, or the Democratic Republic of Congo. Barriers of instability, danger and corruption block the way down this toughest of continents, and the choice is an unpleasant one. Like voting for government, you hold your nose when you choose. Of the three, only Sudan was currently giving out visas with any semblance of regularity. Having already had my route across Asia severed, Sudan seemed my only chance of getting through Africa. I had to get that visa. It is horrible to have your hopes rest on somebody else's whim, especially the whim of a bored, under-paid minion of an oppressive regime. I applied for the visa in Amman because if I was rejected I could travel on to Cairo and try again.

The time waiting in Amman passed swiftly. I met interesting people, and there was festive merrymaking and calorie cramming all round. I enjoyed *iftars* with Jordanian families fasting for Ramadan, and Christmas dinners with ex-pats. For an invitation to the 'British Ball' at a swanky hotel, I hastily borrowed a dinner jacket and a pair of shoes. I chatted with the ambassador and felt out of place as waiters glided by with trays of champagne. But I filled up on the buffet, tucked into the free bar with gusto and escaped the dance floor for a little adventure. I climbed up fire escapes and ladders to the roof of the hotel, high above Amman. Not the loveliest of cities, Amman has too much cheap concrete and hasty building. Sixty years of population growth, Bedouin urbanisation and incoming Palestinian refugees has multiplied the population sixty-fold, but from my rooftop perch the night-time illuminated concrete boxes rolling over Amman's seven hills were beautiful.

When the champagne caught up with me, I awoke, in total darkness, on a toilet seat with my pants around my ankles, and no idea where I was. I felt my way out of the cubicle and stumbled round until I found the exit. As the toilet door opened the bright morning sunlight that filled the foyer of the hotel reminded me with a rush of embarrassment where I was. The party was over. Worse than my fast-emerging hangover was the foolish feeling that I had been fast asleep on a toilet as the party ended and everybody went home. Eyes down, I hurried out of the hotel and crossed Amman in my dinner jacket, nursing my head and cringing at how my hosts would laugh when I got to their house. When I arrived and saw John, fast asleep at the wheel of his car, and still in his dinner jacket, I crept past him and into the house. Everyone was still asleep. I had got away with it! After a quick shower, I took a book and a cup of tea into the garden, and prepared to tease John and his wife for stumbling home hours after I had. Having nothing deeper than temporary friendships is hard, and it meant that I rarely felt able to completely let my guard down. The rigour of courtesy, politeness and tact was a pressing discipline, and so those swift and comfortable friendships that I did find became very precious indeed.

I sat on a low stool in a street café, smoked a *nargileh* water pipe and played backgammon with a wise old man. His parents gave up the nomadic desert life when he was a boy, and came to live in the city. He bought me glasses of tea, and in return he had the pleasure of winning several games of backgammon. He threw the dice, one red, one green, onto the board of black wood and pale mother of pearl. "All the four colours of our flag," he observed, exhaling a plume of sweet apple smoke. He spoke of backgammon as a philosophy for life. "It is black and white and you have no choice over what is dealt for you, or over what other people do to you. The choice that you do have is how to best play your own pieces, to make all you possibly can out of what you have been dealt."

My hopes for a Sudanese visa had been miserably low. Sudan had only recently started issuing visas, and travellers' tales abounded of repeated, unpredictable refusals. I was nervous when I dropped my passport at the Embassy. That visa was crucial, but I was pessimistic, almost angry, as I filled in the pages of paper work. It seemed pointless. I fully expected some power-happy, paranoid, good-for-nothing, paperclip shuffling bureaucrat to reject me without a thought or a care. To my massive surprise though, my dice fell well and my application was accepted at the first attempt. The man at the barred window who handed me back my passport was surprised by the force of my enthusiastic handshaking and thanks. He was not even Sudanese. Now I had no reason to bail out. I had the visa, now I had Sudan to tackle. I was scared as well as excited. Slowly and stuttering perhaps, but I was still moving.

My friends arrived. Simon, a keen sailor from Devon, had never really cycled before. He had emailed me with his rather unorthodox preparations. "Al: I am in pain! Please don't tell anyone! Someone advised me to shave my bum to make cycling less painful. But now I am sitting on hundreds of tiny, deadly needles of stubble. Please advise…" Arno, the Frenchman, had told me that he planned to cycle to Heathrow Airport with a 6ft cardboard bike-storage box under his arm.

Somehow this pair made their way to Amman. I was excited to have company, and I chattered non-stop as we pedalled out of town together. We passed the crude Palestinian shanty towns, the sheep bleating on fetid piles of rubbish and the flapping, scavenging birds, and rode into the brown countryside. On either side of the road were motionless, staring shepherds and running children. We cycled past Mount Nebo, from where Moses first gazed on the Promised Lande whizzed down to the lowest point on Earth, and stopped to bob and float and giggle in the salty soup of the Dead Sea, 400 metres below sea level. When I met the manager of the 5-star Dead Sea Spa Resort at the British Ball, he had offered his luxurious hospitality. Freshly shampooed and blow-dried, we donned fluffy white dressing gowns, relaxed and gloated. Thus pampered, the three rugged adventurers then left to camp on the seashore.

Across the tranquil waters lay the less tranquil West Bank. So, when Jordanian soldiers found our campsite, they moved us on to go sleep elsewhere. We moved our tents a few hundred metres from the shore. Being Jordanians though, they could not help being friendly and they first let us peer through their night-vision goggles. The West Bank showed up in a creepy grainy-green light. Were equally paranoid soldiers over there squinting back at us, I wondered?

The shore of the Dead Sea was an easy ride. The land was arid, the cliffs striped with reds and creams. Saltpans gleamed. Sheer gorges and *wadis* (ravines or valleys, dry except occasionally in the rainy season) folded back from the shore. Whenever we stopped flies descended on us. The ride back up from the world's lowest spot on land was predictably hard, a 1,400 metres winding climb up to the highway at Tafila. Simon was shattered, not surprising as the only training he had done was to freewheel down to the lowest point on the planet and shave his buttocks.

We ran out of water. Simon was on the verge of 'hitting the wall' when we came across a water truck, irrigating roadside plants. We had barely seen a plant for two days, were desperate for water, and now we came across a tanker watering flowers in the desert! It was a bizarre coincidence and we gratefully refilled our bottles. The workers boiled tea for us on a small fire of twigs, as every Jordanian did at every opportunity. As we drank the tea they used some vivid charades to demonstrate what they would like to do to the Israelis, and what they would like to do to their wives.

We continued down the rolling King's Highway, the road on which the Israelites had been refused permission to pass in the Bible. Except for a few olive groves the land was virtually barren. Shepherd boys sat squinting at us as their goats foraged on the flinty slopes. Outcrops of rocks, *jebels*, were red and rough and, in the distance, smoky blue mountains faded smoothly into the desert floor.

The mountain tops were clear against the sky but their bases merged together into one endless string of peaks, seeming to cross all of Arabia.

We met an Irish conceptual artist at a roadside tea house, in Jordan on an assignment. He was to take 24 photographs with a disposable camera, of Arabs writing Arabic greetings on postcards of London. He would then mail them to another artist in London. The art? Sending a postcard of a place you have never been, to a country you have never seen to a man you have never met, in a language he will not understand.

"Ingenious," I said, disingenuously.

Christmas morning dawned over the staggeringly lovely gorge of Wadi Dana, which drops a vertical mile towards the Dead Sea. Birds circled in the sky below us as we ate *felafel* sandwiches for breakfast. They only cost 10p each and so, as it was Christmas, we treated ourselves to three each. Our bikes were wrapped in tinsel, we were wearing Santa hats and, as we pedalled along the crisp, cool King's Highway we sang carols at the top of our voices. Local Muslims laughed as we passed. "Merry Christmas!", "Papa Noel!", "Happy New Year!", even "Happy Birthday!" they cried.

Corned beef and tomato puree sandwiches made a sumptuous Christmas lunch. We three hungry cyclists were appreciative of all we ate that day. In the afternoon we sought shade in the company of a Bedouin family. We drank hot, sweet tea from delicate glasses in the shade of their tent, reviving the senses and forging friendships. The old Bedouin man swapped his red and white *kiffiyeh* for Arno's Santa hat.

We arrived, hot and tired, in Petra before sunset. Secretly and heroically, Simon had lugged a Christmas pudding and a bottle of port all the way from England, and we celebrated Christmas in style.

In the 1840's, John William Burgon described Petra as: 'the hues of youth upon a brow of woe, which Man deemed old two thousand years ago. Match me such a marvel save in Eastern clime: a rose-red city half as old as time.' The 'lost' city's staggeringly ambitious structures, carved from the rock, were re-discovered by Europeans only in 1812 when brave Johann Burckhardt disguised himself as an Arab and persuaded a local to guide him down the tight, winding canyon, or *siq*, that leads to Petra, claiming that he wanted to sacrifice a sheep there. Today Petra was every bit as beautiful as I had hoped since first watching *Indiana Jones' Last Crusade*.

Petra provoked ambition and far-sightedness. Projects that had taken lifetimes to complete mocked the triviality of our modern lifestyles and our demands for instant gratification. It gave me renewed strength. I could make it to Cape Town.

I was reading TE Lawrence's Seven Pillars of Wisdom and was thrilled to spend three days in the vast natural amphitheatre of Wadi Rumm, a magnificent swathe of blushing desert hemmed in by towering ramparts of rock. I imagined Lawrence and bands of vengeful Arabs, mounted on camels and armed to the teeth, riding silently up that valley, a 'processional way greater than imagination', where I now sat and read Lawrence's words: 'Our little caravan grew self-conscious, and fell dead quiet, afraid and ashamed to flaunt its smallness in the presence of the stupendous hills.'

The timeless silence of Wadi Rumm reminded me of my own minute insignificance. Lying on the valley floor, the black stillness was so absolute that I literally could hear myself blink. Rush hour felt a long way away, and laughably irrelevant. Perhaps overwhelmed with the Big Questions of Life, we shattered the heavy silence, charging through the darkness and doing noisy aeroplane impressions. We cooked marshmallows on the camping stove and smoked and choked on the pipe that Arno had given me for Christmas, saying that no Englishman could aspire to be a famous explorer without a pipe.

The mountainous road, basic food and rough campsites took their toll on my friends and they were both relieved when we reached the Red Sea at Aqaba. I was glad, a little cruelly, to see how hard they found the ride. Welcome to my world, boys! But their company had been invaluable. Riding and chatting through the miles, and drinking cups of sweet tea at sunset beside our tents, they had given me a valuable present. I rediscovered the pleasure of laughter. I hope that, in return, their time on the road had reminded them that you only know your strength once you start to take the strain.

To avoid an Israeli visa stamp, we took the short ferry hop from Aqaba to Nuweiba in Egypt. If I entered Israel, I would be barred from many Islamic countries that I hoped to ride through, and I did not want to risk the old trick of getting the stamps on a loose piece of paper.

We slept on the ferry and woke as we arrived in Egypt.

Soon afterwards I was alone again, and with all of Africa now awaiting.

Amman to Khartoum

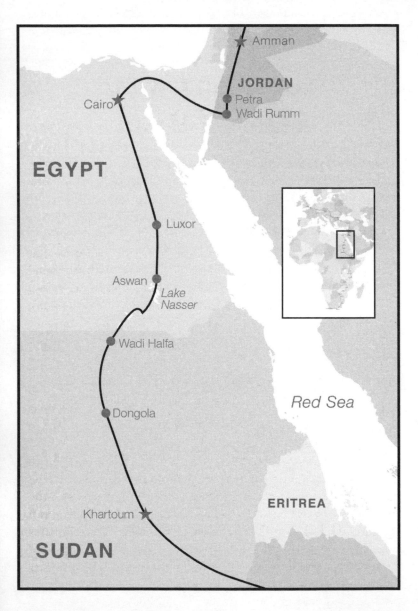

No, I don't want
a Camel Ride!

Denial ain't just a river in Egypt.
Mark Twain

I had almost decided that Yorkshire to Cairo was quite far enough a trek for me to be able to go home with my head held high, when a group called Cycle to the Summit emailed me. They were riding to the Earth Summit in Johannesburg and asked if I would like to join the three of them. Sudan was seeming like an insurmountably frightening prospect when Pedro, a Swiss cyclist with a squint and a big smile hove into view. He had just ridden from Sudan to Egypt and he reassured me about what lay ahead. These two welcome arrivals at such timely moments felt like a small miracle. Whilst God was in this good mood I wondered if he might also send me a beautiful blonde.

I began the New Year riding across the Sinai peninsula to Cairo, battling remorseless headwinds that infuriated me by day and blew down my tent at night. Hailstones stung as I rode through the desert beside two men on camels. They moved on the sand while I rode the long carpet of tarmac. Water bottles froze solid inside my tent. The wind slowed me so much that I ran out of food. A man in a petrol station gave me some dry bread and two onions to keep me going.

I lay on my belly watching the sun set. After three hard days, the wind had calmed. I had hidden my camp out of sight of the road, behind an oil-refinery, and was anxious for the welcome safety blanket of darkness to descend before I was spotted and booted out. The Red Sea stayed copper blue even in the sunset, and the mountains of Sinai blushed purple behind. It would be a very long time before I next saw the sun set over the sea. After sunset, the Gulf sparkled and shone with lights and gas burning from refineries, the darkening sky a livid red bruise. My father had sailed up this Gulf a few decades earlier with the Merchant Navy, and I enjoyed imagining him here. Before my ride I had never paid much attention to Dad's adventures. I had been grateful for his encouragement to follow my own path and his belief in the value of travel, but I never really connected his slides and anecdotes with real, tangible experiences around the globe. Now his experiences became vivid to me.

Arriving in Cairo without a map, I was soon totally lost in the chaos of mad traffic. I wound past mosques, markets, leafy side-streets, neat squares, squalid poverty, smart hotels and the City of the Dead where thousands have made their home in a cemetery amongst the graves and tombs. As I swerved past a slow donkey cart laden with carrots, a black Mercedes almost hit me. I started to think that the traffic was too dangerous for bikes, when a ghostly-looking baker cycled past, covered from head to foot in flour, a tray piled high with fresh bread balanced on his head.

Night began to fall as I reached the banks of the Nile and rode upstream. The Nile, Leigh Hunt mused, 'flows through old hushed Egypt and its sands, like some grave mighty thought threading a dream.' I was surprised how narrow the World's longest river was here. We would be together now for a long time, all the way to Ethiopia. Across the city and through the settling dusk, I saw with a squeeze of excitement, the tops of the pyramids. From the Yorkshire Dales to the pyramids! In a leafy neighbourhood I was gripped by stomach cramps. I leapt a high fence into what turned out to be the dark garden of a swanky riverside restaurant, dropped my pants then leaped back over the fence before any diners saw me or someone nicked Rita. I raced on through the stream of cars, some of which had their headlights on, until, exhausted, windburned and relieved to have survived the Cairo traffic, I arrived at Will and Kathleen Stacey's house, the Principals of Cairo American College. I sat with a Coke in one hand, a beer in the other, and fell asleep.

Cairo is a cauldron of history and amazement. The pyramids are certainly spectacular but were spoiled for me by the throngs of people trying to sell me tacky stuff. It is not a new scourge. Back in 1866 Mark Twain had a similar experience: 'We suffered torture that no pen can describe from the hungry appeals for *baksheesh*.' And William Makepeace Thackeray howled: 'The importunity of these ruffians is a ludicrous annoyance to which a traveller must submit.' Camel rides, T-shirts, 'Where you from? England? Lovely Jubbly, tally ho, have a shifty...' cried the salesmen. The only T-Shirt that tempted me bore the slogan 'NO, I do *NOT* want a Camel Ride!' Disappointing also was the discovery that Cairo has grown so huge that lying just beyond the National Geographic views of the pyramids are rows of grubby KFC's and concrete sprawl. I had to struggle to grasp a sense of wonder.

I decided not to join the *Cycle to the Summit* team riding down to South Africa. Riding with three other people would be more fun, far safer and much easier, but I wanted to at least try to make it on my own. I wanted to find out whether I was up to itith three other foreigners, I would not be able to immerse myself so completely in African life and, as Lawrence said: 'It was a part of pride with Englishmen to hug solitude; ourselves finding ourselves to be remarkable, when there was no competition present.' Throughout my journey ran the constant thread of the rules that I set myself, the standards by which my quest had to stand up to my own harsh self-scrutiny. In some ways my whole journey was strangely contrived and artificial, yet its difficulty sometimes felt even larger by being arbitrary and self-chosen. A man climbing Everest has a clear set of obstacles to overcome: he must cope with cold and danger, and if he does not hurry, then his body will weaken and he will fail, or die. Get to the top. Get back down. Job done. A yachtswoman sailing alone round the world is aware that she has a finite supply of food and a route that she must complete. For me things were less clear. There was no prize, award, trophy or record at stake. My route and journey would be as hard or as easy, as long or as short as I made it. My competition was with myself. I set myself a problem and then had to solve it. It is hard to motivate yourself to build a high brick wall, knowing that you have then to climb over it. It is a strange person too who bangs his head ever harder against that brick wall because he knows that the harder he bangs, the sweeter the stopping will feel.

In the weird, artificial world of carefree westerners seeking fulfilment through pointless physical challenges, there is a yearning to push the boundaries, to seek satisfaction through overcoming ever-greater self-imposed hardships. Edmund Hillary and Tenzing Norgay were the first to climb Everest and live to tell the tale. It was a spectacular achievement. Years later Messner and Habeler struggled to the summit without supplemental oxygen. It was a phenomenally difficult thing to do, yet was their ascent any 'better' than Hillary and Tenzing's? Equally, was it any 'worse' because they were not the first to the summit? Does primacy matter more than personal primacy? If Messner and Habeler are to be applauded for the 'purity' of their achievement should they have climbed the peak stark naked? If we acknowledge that artificial aids, like clothes, tents and crampons are acceptable, then should we not equally applaud Maurice Wilson's plan to crash his plane into the flank of the mountain and simply stroll on up to the summit?

This was the debate I had regularly with myself as I pondered the 'rules' of my private challenge. How pure was my ride to be? It was an infinitesimally graded scale, with no correct answers, and with countless variables. The ride was important to me, to my future, to my self-confidence, to all the hard work I had gone through to get to this point. And yet, I was always wryly aware that it was only a bike ride. It didn't really *matter*. So what if I came home, or rode with some other people, or wildly wasted £1 in a hedonistic Coca-Cola blow out or took a bus one day. It was only a bloody bike ride!

I emailed the *Cycle to the Summit* group with my decision, adding that I hoped that we would meet somewhere so that we could ride together for a few weeks.

After Cairo I had to cycle south along the coast. The police said that I was not allowed to cycle beside the Nile because of 'security concerns'. I was disappointed. The Nile Valley is the beating heart of Egypt and not to ride it meant missing out on so much. My memories of Egypt are isolated and bipolar, limited to Cairo in the North and the southern Upper Nile towns of Luxor and Aswan. I never got a proper feel for Egypt. The Red Sea coast was a half-finished, half-hearted building site, rows of unfinished apartment blocks and hotels, empty windows staring blankly like fish in a market.

Past Hurghada I cut back inland to Luxor. At the first police checkpoint I was stopped. After the shootings of foreign tourists several years before, the Egyptians were still paranoid about their tourism industry. Despite my full repertoire of pleading, smiling, yelling, crying and bribing they were adamant; I could ride no further and I had to hitch a ride with the daily armed convoy. Like many things I was to encounter in developing regions of the world, this convoy defied any rational answer to the question 'Why?' I trained myself over the next years to not ask officials 'Why?' as the answer was usually exasperating. With every wealthy foreign tourist now travelling together in a close convoy at a set time each day it is hard to imagine an easier or juicier target for terrorists. Sadly I heaved my bike onto the back of a lorry and hitched a ride to Luxor. My dream of cycling every inch of the world was broken. The perfect purity of the ride was over. I felt gutted. I would have to settle for a less satisfying goal of 'cycling every inch of the world that was not impeded by a stubborn policeman'. I was then annoyed at myself by how much I enjoyed travelling in the back of the lorry, enjoying the cool breeze and the bright sunshine and the fast effortless miles as I read my book.

But I really was disappointed and so, when they eventually let me out of the lorry, I tried to ride away through the next checkpoint. The soldiers waved at me to stop but I just smiled and waved back, playing the dumb foreigner role for all it was worth. They did not have a vehicle so I thought I might get away with it. They started shouting so I pedalled like crazy. Passing cars were honking me to stop. I played dumb and waved at them too, hammering at the pedals. My freedom lasted a couple of miles before a minibus commandeered by the soldiers swerved in front of me. They were not amused. The soldiers made me take another ride into Luxor itself in a police truck. They then tried to charge me for the ride until I exploded in indignation and they let me off.

The Nile valley was lush green, the sky the deep blue of a late summer's afternoon in England. Swallows dipped the waters and I wondered whether any of them would be visiting my village that summer. Egypt had not inspired me. I was tired of people trying to rip me off every day. I had even found myself looking forward to Sudan but now Egypt was in danger of winning my affections. Luxor soon stopped that, the Nile making a pretty backdrop to Japanese tourists swathed in Egyptian *galibayahs* and a thumping headache of annoying vendors...

"Hello, my friend! Where you from? Stop one minute, can I ask you a question? Just look! No hassle! You wanna taxi ride-felucca ride-horse ride-motor boat ride-drugs ride? You wanna buy waterpipe, t-shirt, galibayah, spices, carpets, genuine antiques, carvings, hashish? Very cheap price! Just for you! Maybe tomorrow? No hassle! My friend, why are you ignoring me?"

Aswan was welcome after Luxor. It was a proper town, filled with normal people and not just the tourist industry. After switching off all my senses in Luxor to cope with the tackiness and hassle I was able in Aswan to be re-amazed by the clothes, the headwear, the leaking pipes and drains, the smells, the wailing but passionate music, the squalor of street-side butchers and fishmongers, the piles of spices and mounds of blue indigo, used for millennia for dying cotton. The land border between Egypt and Sudan has been closed for years so I had to wait for the weekly ferry across Lake Nasser, the largest artificial lake in world, past the extraordinary temples of Abu Simbel – physically relocated in the 1960's when Lake Nasser was formed – and into Sudan.

I killed time in pavement cafés, drinking glass after glass of tea, smoking waterpipes and thinking for hours about Sudan. I emailed friends and family and checked football scores on the internet. I sat by the river and watched the graceful feluccas, wooden boats with white sails like birds' wings. The sails fluttered slowly as the boats tacked through the wind. Unsure which was worse when trying to sleep, an uncomfortable bed, mosquitoes, close proximity to a late night disco, even closer proximity to a mosque's very early wake-up call, or a flock of cockerels outside, I played safe and got them all. The only consolation to the hostel was a beautiful Turkish girl with almond eyes, luminous like a cat's, which mesmerised me. She rolled round my mind for many miles to come.

I bought a pile of flat bread from a baker's oven on the street. Scalding hot in my hands I juggled my way back to the hostel. I was nervous and excited. The ferry was leaving today. This was make or break time. If I could make it through Sudan I could make it through Africa, and if I could make it through Africa, I could make it through anything. I packed up my bags and cycled to the port.

Packing

Every increased possession loads us with new weariness.
John Ruskin

Everything I own is in the faded bags that I carry on my bike. I could list every one of my possessions. Wherever I go, all day, every day, I have to carry them. Four waterproof panniers – two red, two black – clip on racks alongside my bike wheels. On top of the rear rack is a spare tyre and my tent, sleeping bag and tiny camping mattress in a blue waterproof canoeing bag, held down by a pair of elastic bungee cords. At least, it used to be waterproof. Like most of my well worn things, it has seen better days and has been repaired with one of my most invaluable possessions – duct tape. I need everything that I own. I no longer have underwear, for instance. You don't need underwear.

My clothes go in one pannier, more or less of them depending on the climate. I ride in the same clothes every day and have a cleaner t-shirt and trousers for days off. To protect myself from the sun and to look as little of a freak as possible, I ride in trousers and a long-sleeved shirt. The other clothes double as a pillow when I camp. Another pannier carries my cooking gear, the stove, petrol bottle, mug, pan, a plastic plate that doubles as a chopping board and pan lid, a spoon, food and water. The front right pannier, the easiest to access, holds what I use regularly during the day: the map, diary, camera, music, pump, basic tools and a book. The final pannier, my 'pannier of doom' is loaded with stuff I rarely use but still need to haul around with me. This is the weight I begrudge the most and I am always looking for ways to cut it down. It includes a battery charger, essential documents, first aid kit, longer-term spare parts that I know I will need before I next reach a bike shop, such as a chain, derailleur, brake blocks, a bottom bracket and spokes. There are also usually a couple of spare books in there. Books are my biggest weakness. Finally, a small bag clips to the handlebar. This carries things that I need while I am actually riding: sunglasses, gloves, hat, suncream, lypsyl and snacks.

The focusing effect of having to carry all of my belongings helps me keep my life uncluttered. Except when loaded with food and water for several days, or equipment for extreme cold, I am able to pick up every thing that I own in the world and carry it. I really value how few things I really need to survive, and I discovered that I actually enjoy the simplicity of owning very little.

Laughing with Allah

God made the Sudan and then He laughed!
Sudanese proverb

Loading the boat on the shore of Lake Nasser was farcically disorganised. Sweating workers yelled at each other and got in each other's way for hour after hot hour, heaving their loads around. The gangplanks and jetty were packed solid with sacks waiting to be loaded. Heavy sacks were dumped on top of boxes of soft fruit, rainbows of stacked plastic chairs were jumbled amongst split bags of sugar. Someone had raided an industrial-sized box of chocolate wafers. The irate captain stormed about, clouting workers round the head as they strained and shouted amongst the never-shrinking mountain of cargo on the dock. Watching, it was hard to imagine that those men do this same thing every week, yet never introduce any method into the madness. This was another unhelpful train of thought – like asking 'why?' – that never failed to irritate me in the developing world.

I heaved Rita through the scrum and seized possession of a small strip of bare deck. It would be my home for the next twenty four hours, plus however long the weekly debate raged over how best to move a sack through a door, and the sailors on the dock shouted at the African Nations football tournament showing on the television. I was ready to defend my space from encroaching piles of cargo, and from the fat man who I suspected of raiding the chocolate wafers. If I should die in the crush, think only this of me...

Below deck, the steel ship was noisy and crowded with extremely dark-skinned Sudanese people, very different to the Arabic Egyptians. There were high cheek-boned women in bright robes and men in white robes with tribal scars. Already the toilet floors were covered in poo. We hadn't even set sail yet. The inviting blue Nile water became ever less so as people chucked rubbish, empty boxes and used nappies overboard.

The sun set. Night fell. The moon rose. Eventually the shouting and the tumult died down. The captain and his ship were ready to depart. It was 9.30pm, we were only six and a half hours late, and I was pleased. I had anticipated worse. Among the old suitcases and cardboard boxes tied with string, squashed hot families shrieked, played dominos, slept, ate, stretched, scratched and simply sprawled, comatose. The temperature and the stench rose. Food was served in the galley by a filthy man, with an apron shiny with grease, fag ash sprinkling into the food like an Italian chef seasoning with oregano. His vast belly was testimony that he probably never ate his own vile cooking. A tin tray was banged on the counter, and the chef scooped a handful of grey chopped tomatoes, a handful of grey boiled beans, a grey egg and half of a, surprisingly orange, orange onto it. Ladies and Gentlemen, dinner is served. I climbed back on deck to escape the heat, noise and stench. Ahead of me lay a land that was a refuge of terrorists, where the government had, until recently, kept tourists away while civil war and ethnic cleansing raged unchecked. But I was no longer scared. I had overcome the nervous inertia of anxious waiting, so the toughest part had been achieved already. I was in motion now. With the simple purity of Newtonian physics, I would stay in motion until acted upon by external forces. I was on my way. The night sky was beautiful. Egypt was only a memory now. Come on, Sudan; let's see what you've got.

I was excited as the ferry docked in Sudan. I felt that the next few weeks would determine the rest of the journey: could

I cross the desert, would I make it safely through this unstable nation? My questions would soon be answered one way or the other. As Frederic Manning said: 'One must try: one is not bound to succeed.' After completing a sheaf of disembarkation paperwork I pedalled through the sand from the customs point to the village of Wadi Halfa and found a place to camp.

That evening most villagers were clustered outside a café around a tiny television to watch a football match between Brazil and Saudi Arabia. Loyalties seemed torn between cheering their Islamic brothers or supporting the inevitable victors. The air was warm and still and the conversation around the café sounded loud and unnatural, surrounded by the stillness of the desert. At a street stall I ate *felafel* and what the vendor described to me as 'Kentucky Fried Fish'. I tried, with the help of my map and the *felafel* chef, to establish where I could resupply with water in the desert ahead. But, before I could begin to ride I had to pass through more immigration checks, register with the police and obtain a permit to travel. This all involved being waved vaguely in the direction of many different identical little offices in search of many different identical little stamps, signatures, counter stamps, confirmatory signatures, payments, stapling and bewildered expressions.

I knew that this bureaucratic labyrinth would take time to negotiate, so I began my quest early in the morning. At the first small office they told me: "Come back at 12.30 when there is electricity so that we can photocopy your passport." From there I went to the tiny bank, and found that it had closed for the day at 12.30. I returned the next morning, filled in a form, and then went to customs where I had to buy a pink folder to hold all the forms, and complete three more forms. One of these was an application for a travel permit, the others were tests of patience. The holder of a travel permit 'must report to police HQ within twenty four hours of arrival in any town to discuss the programme of his visit,' I discovered. Already frustrated by the bureaucracy I ignored this demand throughout Sudan and nobody ever cared.

I moved on to the small window at the 'Aliens' building, where I was required to buy another pink folder. But first I had to find the officer: he was in a nearby café. The next form required the purchase of an additional stamp. The price was clearly labelled as 300 dinar (75p), but I had to pay 400 (£1). The man at the desk shrugged at my protests, as if to say: 'Look, you need a stamp, I have the stamps. You either pay the money or you don't get a stamp. I don't care which you do, just realise that I am holding all the aces. And the stamps.' He had an expressive shrug.

In another office, much careful stapling and gluing was required before I moved to a further office where a signature had to be sought out. Successful, I proceeded to another office for a stamp and two more forms, which the official kindly completed for me, though excruciatingly slowly. Ah, but he had run out of stamps. I paid 7,100 dinar and went to a different office for the stamp. They required 200 dinar more. I returned to the office of the Big Cheese. He sent me into a scrum at a small window. I gave 100 dinar to the face at the window and returned to the office. I had no idea what I was paying for anymore. I was passed on to another man, who was praying. I waited. Then the Big Cheese began to pray. The other man returned. Was this to be the elusive final stamp I was searching for…? He stamped the stamp. Ah, but no, this was not the end. On to another office for another signature. Back to the previous office. There the folders were carefully filed in a big black filing cabinet where nobody would ever look at them again. And at long last the policeman turned to me with a smile. I had reached the end of the maze.

I had a permit to travel as far as Khartoum and I was registered to be in Wadi Halfa. After many hours penance as a bureaucrats' pinball, I was free to properly enter Sudan. I would ride south to Khartoum, and then southeast into Ethiopia. The government were reluctant to allow any tourists into Sudan, and certainly would not allow me anywhere near southern Sudan, a land struggling to recover from decades of civil war. Neither could I travel to the tragic west of the country, where desperately poor people suffered famine and neglect, discrimination, murder and ethnic cleansing at the hands of the government.

I climbed a small hill to watch the sunset, exhausted. The blue waters of man-made Lake Nasser seemed an invasion in this end-of-the-world, needle-in-a-haystack, middle-of-nowhere kind of place, bringing colour, a ferry and a weekly splash of activity into the silence of the desert. Wadi Halfa was a sandy settlement with no paths or roads, no trees, no colours, no contours. It was featureless like snowfall. Which route would I take across the desert? Around the village was a tangle of tracks but I could not see any leading south out of town past the low rocky hills. Wadi Halfa is an odd place to have on a list of my world 'highlights': a few clusters of square, drab, single-storied dwellings. But it is a highlight because it was the most remote place I had ever been to at the time and making it there gave me a boost of much-needed confidence. I paused to remember and to thank all the people who had, over the years, got me to that small hill in a torpid backwater at the northern tip of the largest country in Africa.

By happy coincidence the *Cycle to the Summit* (C2S) team, complete with a new-found fourth member, had been on the same ferry as me and I decided to ride for a while with them. I worried that by not tackling the desert alone I was taking the easy way out, but in the end I decided that the pleasure of having company was more important at the moment than my constant instinct to make life difficult for myself. The desert would still be hot and sandy, if just a little more crowded.

Ruth, the only woman of the team, had come up with the idea of cycling to the Earth Summit in Johannesburg, the World Summit on Sustainable Development, in order to raise the profile of Water Aid, an international charity dedicated to helping people escape the stranglehold of poverty and disease caused by living without safe water and sanitation. Tough and intelligent, Ruth's Irish burr reminded me of a young Dervla

Murphy. Toby was the organisational driving force and the mouthpiece for the project. An entertaining, relaxed character, he did not enjoy cycling very much. Paul was several years older than the rest of us. Quiet and good-natured, he was a good mechanic, a fan of big engines, and the only cyclist I have ever met with a 6-foot yoga mat strapped to the back of his bike. He often disappeared in villages to examine water pumps and old cars. Owy, an Australian, was the new-found fourth member of the team. Working in a Thai restaurant in Edinburgh, he had seen an advert the team had posted after the original fourth man quit to return to his girlfriend, just a few weeks into the ride. So Owy had packed his bags and flown to Cairo for a crack at riding through Africa. An appalling dancer and a lively soul, Owy and I amused ourselves with events like desert follow-my-leader on the bikes and long jump competitions in the readily available sand.

The C2S team's professional-looking solar panels, laptop computer and sponsored bikes were evidence of good preparation, and reminded me of the broken promises and merry-go-round certain people and companies had led me on before I started. Their attempts at cooking or putting up tents, however, were decidedly amateur and made me feel much better about my shabby equipment. They travelled slow and easy, took at least two hours to pack up in the mornings, rode slowly and ate well. Their magnificent lunchtime picnics of tuna and cheese and chocolate were a depressing contrast to my bread and jam diet. Jam yesterday and jam tomorrow, and jam today as well. Alice in Wonderland would have been jealous, but I was sick of it. Bread and jam every day then pasta with a stock cube for dinner. My culinary highlights were a new box of stock cubes or a new flavour of jam. Their relaxed way of travel was a contrast to my militaristic, ascetic masochism, and I welcomed the chance to calm down and relax.

We wobbled and bounced across the sand towards Khartoum. The track was rutted like a washboard, an infuriating feature of dirt roads, common whenever vehicles drive on soft dirt surfaces. Our bikes were heavy with water and food gathered from Wadi Halfa's few tiny market stalls. A final police checkpoint scrutinised our travel permits, checked that we had sufficient food and water and then released us out into the desert. I thought of WC Fields crossing a desert in more civilised days: 'It took us a week to cross the desert. Things got so bad we had to drink water.'

Before long my backside was bruised, my spine felt compressed by several inches and my neck was whip-lashed by the corrugated 'road'. I had never experienced anything like it before. When the rattling became too much, I would venture into the sand in search of smoother ground. But when the bike hit soft sand my legs span wildly as the tyres skidded and I slewed uncontrollably for lack of traction. Direction of travel became entirely random and less important than simply keeping moving, because once you stopped you could not easily get started again and had to walk with the bike until you reached firmer ground.

When the sand was too deep to ride we pushed our heavy bikes, laden with three days supply of food and water. Even pushing the bike was sometimes too hard and then we had to pull the loads instead. Arse-first was a ludicrous way to be crossing a continent. We were drenched with sweat and our heads thumped with the heat. It was every man for him- or herself, as we searched for rideable terrain. Spinning wildly away from the impassable soft sand we would all career off in our own directions searching for elusive patches of firm black gravel. We fanned out so far one day that we lost Toby and Owy in the broken landscape of rock-pile hillocks and dunes. Interwoven trails, tyre tracks, donkey tracks, camel tracks, footprints and flip -lop tracks wove all over the land, around the occasional villages that punctuated our way. Occasionally small buses passed, roaring and straining at the sand, their engines protesting, hordes of passengers clinging to the sides and roof. Away from the villages we would see nothing all the way to the horizon, perhaps just a few bushes to take a bearing on or an occasional hint of the Nile, shimmering green away to the right. We had to haul ourselves over low dunes, my trousers tearing and shoes filling with sand. Our relative speeds varied enormously, and at times we were all out of one another's sight for hours on end. Edward Gibbon wrote that he was 'never less alone than when completely alone'. He had clearly never hauled a bike through miles of shimmering sand, alone as far as the horizon in every direction, over a flat and featureless brown-pink blancmange, dusted with chocolate shards of hard black rock. The blood roared through my head and stars danced on my eyeballs. Even my singing failed to break the sense of silence.

For two punishing weeks we dragged and pushed the bikes in 45°C heat. The dawns and dusks were a refreshing relief from the punching power of the daytime sun. Unable to wash, we were permanently grimed with sweat and sand, and I was smiling wildly. Rivulets of sweat ran white stripes down our dirty faces, and our clothes were crusty and ringed with salt. It was physically gruelling, but I was in my element at last. Teaching Biology in Oxford seemed a wonderfully long way away. This was what I had left home for.

At night a hot wind blew, shaking the scraps of vegetation that hugged the small waterholes where camels roared their strangled, bubbling cries, and we slept. I lay on my back in the sand, my blistered lips cracked into a smile. The stars looked more exotic through the mosquito net hanging down over me from my bicycle, and for the first time on the journey I saw the Southern Cross, my favourite constellation. The bottom half of the world was no longer so far away. The ground was scattered with stones that glowed in the dark if you knocked them together. Barefoot in the desert of Sudan, I was so happy. At first light I would watch the day break over the Nile as the bag of night burst, and gold spilled over the world. On Valentine's Day I woke at sunrise. No postman bore gifts from secret admirers. Even 6,000 miles from home, some things did not change.

We rode past a memorial to the British soldiers killed in the Anglo-Egyptian campaign of the 1880's. As I stood before the smashed plinth I wondered what those young soldiers thought of this harsh land, as they fought and died for Queen and country so far from home.

One night we camped on a wide scenic bend of the Nile. My yearning to jump in and swim was just outweighed by my fear of crocodiles. Toby, braver, dumber, or maybe more hygienic than I, took his chances and survived. Swallows dipped the water and a flock of roosting birds made a racket in the haven of an acacia tree. Across the river a village sang and danced to rhythmic drums. After dark I went with Owy and Toby down to the riverbank to try and spot crocs with our torches. A couple of loud splashes sent us scampering back to our camp, our eyes like golf balls.

We reached a village every two or three days, small clusters of huts with cheerful, colourfully painted doors. Arriving we would often see a hanging animal skin filled with water: a symbolic welcoming gesture as water is so important for desert travellers. Islamic hospitality is always generous. Rather than sharing things as Christians are supposed to do, Muslims are taught to give everything away. Add to that the traditional hospitality of desert peoples and you arrive at the incredible generosity of the Sudanese. In El Kandak a man invited us into his home for breakfast. This sort of spontaneous kindness was a regular occurrence. This family were holding a wedding feast in their home that very afternoon, but seemed quite relaxed about five filthy foreigners descending on their home just a few hours before the wedding began. Back home a wedding morning brings high panic, but the Sudanese are wonderfully lacking in agitation. They fed us meat on top of a pile of rice, on top of a pile of soggy bread, and we gratefully stuffed it into our mouths with our fingers. All around us women worked feverishly at preparing the wedding feast. The man, Mohammed, left the wedding arrangements in the capable hands of his womenfolk and took us to see the stately police building built by the British in 1902 and a crumbling mud-walled fortress where we amused ourselves by locking Toby in the jail.

The village of Abri felt like an Eden on the riverbank because the market sold fresh fruit and vegetables. Owy, struck by constipation for days, was particularly delighted. The vegetable stall was shaded by a large green tree that trembled in the breeze, seeds shaking in their long pods. Two ladies leaned on the stall, relaxed, their hair wrapped in crimson cloth. Pyramids of tomatoes and potatoes and bunches of carrots were tied together with their bushy greenery. A fruit we ate regularly in Sudan, but never learned the name of, always had to be cut in half before eating so that you could blow away the tiny flies that lived in the middle.

I loved riding through the villages, between whitewashed walls on the single sandy street, corners smoothed by age and carefree workmanship. The only reminder that this was the 21st century was the constant flap-flap sound of the water pumps down at the river pumping water to irrigate the small vegetable fields. Men and women would laugh and wave kindly at us. Children shouted, "How-are-you? How-are-you? What-is-your- name? What-is-your-name?" yet understood not a word of our replies. In one village school we heard a class singing, "Everyday I wash my face. Everyday I clean my nose..."

The bicycles of Sudan put mine to shame with their splendid decorations: frames striped with coloured electrical tape and a cornucopia of aerials, bells, laser beam noise machines, wing mirrors (at least four), large mud flaps (mud? in Sudan?) and with flourishes of dangly stuff and jangling Pepsi caps, strips of cardboard against the spokes to produce a motorcycle sound effect, frilly things in the wheels, tassels on the seats and often a huge chrome headlamp (broken). They were normally ridden by small boys who could barely straddle the crossbar let alone sit on the saddle.

Arriving in Sudan it had taken less than a day for my fears about Sudan and its people to evaporate and I felt perfectly at ease in the country. They were the friendliest, kindest people that I had ever met, filled with warmth and laughter. Invitations for tea and gifts of dates were never-ending, spontaneous, and genuine. The old sage who said: 'God made the Sudan and then He laughed!' meant it as a slight, but I saw a Sudan full of laughter.

The midday heat was unbearable so we would find excuses to delay, chatting for hours in villages until late afternoon, lingering over sweet tea in the mottled shade of woven grass awnings. The others would intrigue the ever-present crowds with their video camera, solar panels and water filters. I never liked the role of Fascinating Rich Foreign Person, and usually took great pains to highlight the similarities in our lives rather than the differences. But digital cameras were far more fun to the villagers of northern Sudan than my philosophies, and I relished the peace and quiet when everybody ignored me. Often though children would creep to my side and watch in quiet fascination as I wrote in my diary. Writing in a funny alphabet and from *left to right* across the page! We were equally mesmerised by each other's lives.

We sat one day at a shaded table in a village café, with our huge pile of bread supplies in front of us. A passing man came and asked how much the bread cost. He must have thought we were selling bread. Joking, I showed him a banknote that was double the normal bread price. He shrugged, took out his money, paid me, and took away a bag of our bread. Everyone in the café roared with laughter, delighted at the foreigners, the *cawadja*, making such a profitable start to their business.

Old men, dressed in white robes and turbans, played dominoes in the shade, their faces lined like the sun-baked earth. I had never thought of dominoes as a noisy sport, but in Sudan it verged on full contact, the pieces slammed down hard amongst much yelling, shouting and hand waving. Women seemed more confident and less like second-class citizens in Sudan than in other Islamic nations, and at one water pump we enjoyed a conversation with a group of women about the state of our hygiene, our filthy faces and torn clothes. Despite the language barrier the message was clear: we were revolting.

After days and days of desert quiet arriving in the small town of Dongola was unsettling. Out of silence into the crowds of white robes and turbans, visions of noisy ghosts. Small donkeys were the main means of transport, bearing heavy loads and fat men. There were some taxis and they carried brightly painted shovels on their roofs for digging themselves out of deep sand. At a tea stall a dark young woman was swathed in indigo blue, ceremonial scars framing her beautiful white eyes. She looked at me and through me, her haughty dignity and poise challenging me, forcing me to lower my eyes and break her gaze that bore deep into my mind. She presided proudly over her small tea stall, her henna tattooed hands gracefully working from her billowing robes. She worked methodically and carefully: rinse the small glasses, add a large spoonful of sugar to each, fan the coals deftly, glowing red bright beneath her hands, add a scoop of tea leaves to a small plastic sieve then half fill each glass from the kettle through the sieve, the chestnut liquid misting the tops of the glasses as tiny jewels of condensation ran back down into the dark sweet tea. The second half of the glass was filled with hot water, a money-saving dilution encountered regularly. The whole simple process was laced with splendour and grace. She had no change and so my change was received in the form of another cup of tea. I paid for the tea, the price negotiated between us by drawing Arabic numerals with our fingers in the sugar bowl. The deal sealed, I dug my spoon into the sugar.

Sometimes I fear that I claim things to be tough when perhaps it was just me being weak. So I was able to derive some grim satisfaction when the frame of Rita snapped after a bruising stretch of ferocious rocky riding. I wiggled the jagged steel tubing masochistically like a wobbly tooth, waved goodbye to the others and then started walking. I walked hard, thinking through the options available to me. I was potentially in big difficulties. Fortunately though I reached the village of Delgo and with a bit of miming and acting tried to find a welder. But the welder was away in Khartoum. I kept walking and in the next village found Mohammed, a bed maker, cookie maker and welder. He was thrilled at the chance to help me out. I did not dare to watch as he casually set to work with his welding torch (shielding his eyes against the flare only with his hand), so I shared tea on the ground with Mohammed's children. Unfortunately bike metal is far thinner than bed metal and Mohammed began by blasting a large hole in the frame. He gasped the Arabic version of 'whoops!' He managed to patch up the hole and fixed on a splint for good measure too. Afterwards he loaded me with cookies, refused payment for the welding and waved me off with a smile. I could not believe how easy it had all been! I rode away at top speed, bursting with relief. By following their tyre tracks I caught the others up at their evening camp by the river. The welding was crude, but it held for a couple of days before it broke again, and I was able to continue on to Khartoum by pausing every few days for the weld to be re-welded. The break looked ever more like a big blob of silver bubble gum, but it held.

Eventually we reached the oft-dreamed of tarmac road that would sweep us in three easy days into Khartoum where I would leave the others. A car stopped ahead of us and out climbed four very fat men. One of them was wearing aftershave. After three weeks without a shower, and surrounded by four almost equally grotty friends, it smelt giddyingly strong and clean. The men gave us four litres of iced water and two litres of 7-Up. My clothes were held together with duct tape and safety pins, and my back was black with flies. I appreciated their generosity.

Eager to reach Khartoum and rest, Toby, Owy and I rode on into the night. We rode bare-chested in the warm night, beneath an amazing display of shooting stars with a large moon high above us. We reached Khartoum as the yolk-like sun began sliding up into the frying pan sky. We had made it! We strode into Khartoum's five star hotel as Toby had heard a rumour that they would serve you beer if you asked confidently enough. He even put on his clean shirt to ask. Unfortunately there was no beer, but they did give us a free fruit juice when we explained our ride. We sat, stinking, at the gleaming bar and toasted each other. The desert crossing I had been so anxious about was behind me now.

My clothes were festering and torn to shreds. My bike had snapped. I was sick of mouldy bread and jam. I longed to hear music once more. 'It is necessary to be cut off from civilization and all that it means to enable you to realise fully the power music has to recall the past, or the depths of meaning in it to soothe the present and give hope for the future,' Cherry Garrard wrote. But even as my kind host from the International School in Khartoum tactfully pointed me towards the shower, I could feel the relief of success. As the dust and sweat pooled around my feet in the shower, I thought of the warmth and grace of a charming people, the privilege of silent sunrises over the Nile, and the satisfaction of lying on my back in the hot sand, sun baked and filthy, a cracked smile on my grubby face in the gritty desert wind.

Heaven in Sudan came in the form of a swimming pool, to dive in and glide through the pale blue quiet with the cool swilling in my ears and eyes. I felt my body and my mind unwinding and relaxing with relief at having made it through to Khartoum so comfortably. I wrestled with bureaucracy, scrummaging through farcically chaotic offices to extend my Sudanese visa, paying lots of money and sitting for many hours in the Ethiopian Embassy applying for a visa, the time passing less painfully thanks to the latest Harry Potter book I had borrowed. For the Ethiopians, my British passport was not sufficient proof that I was actually British. I had to take my British passport to the British Embassy where they glanced at it, typed on a piece of paper, 'is British,' or something equally insightful, and cheerily charged me 40 quid.

I left a note there for a man who, I had been told, could find you a beer in Khartoum. Alcohol had been banned by President Numeiry in 1983, and all alcohol stocks ceremoniously dumped in the Nile. Correspondingly, invitations for the evenings at the Embassy bar, known as the Pickwick Club, were jealously guarded. But I managed to wangle one. Boddingtons beer and darts in a mock pub felt very odd in the heat, but in a country where beer was hard to find, I made the most of it. At closing time I was hauled along to another party at the home of a British oil executive. His three-storey mansion was flowing with booze, hazy with pot smoke and patrolled by five live-in prostitutes dressed in Gucci. But the real excitement was the news that somebody had just returned from Kenya with a box of fresh mushrooms, unavailable in Sudan. I had not realised that I had been missing mushrooms until I smelt them cooking. I eagerly joined the salivating throng jostling around the sizzling pan. The oil man chatted with me about my journey and invited me to stay in his mansion – on-tap whores and all – for as long as I wanted. I politely declined. Decadent extravagance, fun though it was, would have felt uncomfortable after the simple circumstances of all the kind Sudanese people I had met.

The contrasts of the people that I met on my ride was fascinating. One of the many special experiences of travelling by bike is that you are in complete contact with the world you ride through. I wanted to experience the world as the people I met experienced it. In poor regions I ate simple food and drank water from wells. And in rich places I ate lobster and enjoyed it equally. You do not present a threatening image on a bicycle, people are less likely to be intimidated by you, and more likely to be intrigued, amused, pitying and welcoming. So I stayed with scores of families. Strangers who invited me into their home and became friends. The variety was staggering. Mud huts and mansions united by similar human feelings. I always worried about being a nuisance or a bore or a leech. It was always reassuring when a family I stayed with 'passed me on' to another friend elsewhere. But, and I cringe a little even now in case I am wrong, the people I met seemed to enjoy the random visitor, passing through their lives. We tend to think of the world as a selfish and unfriendly place, and forget that it is only a collection of ordinary individuals, just like ourselves. The inherent goodness of almost everybody I met was the overwhelmingly dominant impression I took away from my ride round our world. That, and the random events that led to me meeting so many strangers and becoming their friend, was one of the biggest enjoyments of my journey.

I met a very strong woman in Khartoum, and listened with horrified awe and respect to her story. Like so many, Rebecca had suffered in the atrocious war in the south of Sudan. After her village was destroyed by government forces, she walked for 75 days with her young children in the hope of finding a better life in Khartoum. Upon reaching the capital she built a new home with her own hands, but the government soon knocked it down. Her husband abandoned her and was later thrown into prison, so Rebecca had been sleeping on the street with her children. She had recently found a new small plot of land and was beginning once again to rebuild her home and her life. Like so many in Africa, she was a woman of substance and her good-humoured heroism and courage made me feel very spoiled and self-pitying.

In a similar vein, I was eager to meet the people working in Sudan with Hope and Homes for Children. I went to visit some of their small family homes in Khartoum. Giggling and shielding their faces behind freshly scrubbed hands, six small boys stood in a group to sing a song for me. The boys were part of a family now, hence the embarrassed performance, the clean faces, enforced best behaviour and uncomfortable Sunday clothes. But these irritations were trivial, because they had a family.

Hope and Homes for Children work to find orphaned or abandoned children an ordinary family home, and to give them as normal a life as possible, helping them to catch up with their school work and to learn trades and skills, relevant and realistic, that will allow them to become independent adults. A year ago these children were on the streets, victims and survivors of the decades of mayhem in the south. They had been rounded up by the government and dumped in one of the camps for Internally Displaced People, their parents just another of the two million people who had disappeared or been killed in the conflict. Alone in the world the children had received scant education, inadequate food and shelter and little love or personal attention for most of their short lives.

Now *Hope and Homes for Children* has worked to provide them with as normal an upbringing as possible, taking them from the shocking government camps and placing them in small foster families. It is nothing fancy or extravagant, it is just a childhood. Now, with a home, school, stability and a family, these children have the chance to re-start their lives. I knew that it was supposed to be me who was helping them, but as I shook their small hands and looked into their shy eyes it was with a feeling of 'you are amazing. I will strive towards your strength, guts, hope, courage and laughter.' A beginning with no schooling, home or parents is out of my comprehension and I drew so much strength and resolve from them.

My three weeks in Khartoum were busy whilst I waited for my visa. I taught PE for a week at the American School, during which time I valiantly, yet vainly, tried to bring cricket into the lives of the Sudanese and ex-pat American children. I had lunch with an Englishman called Edmund who had recently bought a camel. I went to a wedding between a French man and a Dinka woman. Amidst much drumming, ululating and brandishing of feathered canes and, inexplicably, a string-less badminton racket, long speeches were made, the essence of which appeared to be that the groom should not dare even consider getting divorced, that the Sudanese should be given French visas more easily, and attempts to convince the family of the Dinka woman that marrying a Frenchman was not a complete disgrace. I met a Sudanese soap opera star and got his autograph. I arranged for Specialized in England to replace my broken bike, and I persuaded my friend Rob to come and join me for 10 days riding in Ethiopia. I would meet them both, Rob and the new bike, in Gondar.

Khartoum to Nairobi

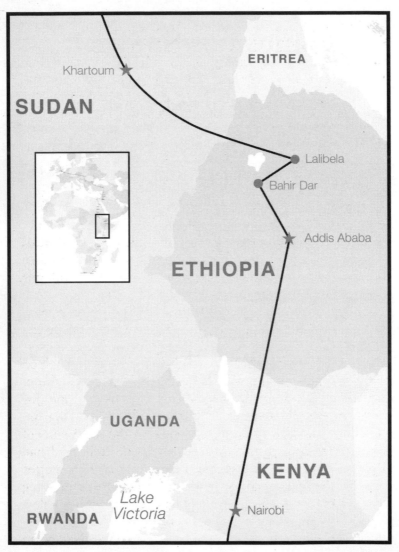

Miles not Smiles

That which does not kill us, makes us stronger.
slogan for the Egyptian Beer, Stella

Once more, I smiled and waved, promised that I would be careful, rang my little bell and then pedalled out of the lives of my new friends. Rounding that first corner, I would be a stranger once more. Nobody would know my name and I would know no-one. I went through my now traditional ritual of crying, feeling sorry for myself, wanting to go home, and then cheering up and enjoying being free once more, wondering what adventures the next stage would hold.

It did not take long to leave Khartoum, but by the time I was on the open road I was already drenched in warm, salty sweat. My long-sleeved blue shirt and baggy grey cotton trousers darkened. After crossing the desert it was a joy to be back on tarmac, to glide out of town and be able to look around rather than having to concentrate on the ground in front of me. Joy is relative, though, and this joy was relatively small. I was on a mission. I needed to hurry to Gondar in the mountains of northern Ethiopia, in time to meet my friend Rob. So I had to put in some serious distance: I aimed for 200 kilometres a day for the first few days. It was too hot to be hammering down a monotonous black stripe of tarmac over wilting yellow plains. My thermometer had a fit, raced off the top of the scale (50°C) and refused to come back down. Ahead of me on the road, enticing me cruelly, was a shining silver pool. Delicious cool waters gleaming. The torture of mirages. A grimy lorry rose silently from the shallows, growing larger as it approached until it careered past with a careless battering of furnace-hot wind and a lungful of oily smoke and desert grit. In the heavy heat the black fumes sagged onto the soft tarmac.

At sunset I crossed the Blue Nile, which wasn't very blue. I would not see her again before Ethiopia. Two flashing white skeins of birds skimmed in 'V' formations over the water, silver-green in the calm evening light. Fretting and calling, they urged each other on in a headlong hurry to somewhere. I left the river and rode through the cooling night until my bike computer finally ticked over 200 kilometres for the day. I pulled off the road and lay down heavily beside my bike on the grey sand, too tired to even unpack my sleeping bag. I woke chilled before dawn. "Too hot, too cold; seems I'm never bloody happy," I grumbled as I got sleepily back on the bike. The temperature rose with the sun, and soon my face set into its daily grimace of pain, wind, heat and intrinsic ugliness. Even my teeth were hot and my eyeballs felt as though they were cooking. The water in my bottles was horribly hot.

Around each small settlement were colourful plastic bag fields, flapping gaily in the wind. Africa is facing a plague of flapping plastic. Every purchase you make comes in a plastic bag, multicoloured and flimsy. Discarded carelessly they blow on the breeze until they snag on scruffy thorns and bushes where they will struggle and squirm for eternity. I stopped to buy bread from a small, gloomy shop. An old calendar was stuck skewed on the rough, unpainted wall with toenail-yellow sticky tape, alongside a lurid green and gold excerpt from the Koran. My eyes took time to focus in the cool gloom. Large sacks of sugar, salt and *chai* were flopped in one dusty corner beside a scoop and a battered set of weighing scales. The store keeper greeted me warmly, expressed the usual surprise at my appearance and waddled outside into the white light to poke and fiddle with my bike. Like every male in Africa he displayed his virility and mechanical prowess by thumbing the pressure of my tyres. He nodded approvingly at their firmness. Eventually he remembered to sell me some bread. Declining the proffered plastic bags I limbo danced with my awkward load from shop to bike, spilling a steady trail behind me. A consolation of buying old, stale bread is that dropping it on the ground does not make it much less palatable.

Small whirlwinds whipped through the villages. Plastic bags and grey sand whistled along and the men's white robes leapt up in Mexican waves. Turbans flapped into disarray. The land was completely flat, and the arrow straight road seemed intent on dropping off the end of the world. Apart from the occasional lorry, the world was silent. I rode steadily onwards.

At the regular police checkpoints my passport was thoroughly examined. I put a great deal of effort into acquiring my travel permit and a photography permit, which warned, openly, that photographing 'examples of poverty or anything that reflects badly on the government is absolutely forbidden.' Yet nobody ever checked them. The novelty of a foreign passport intrigued them, though. The policemen clearly had no idea what they were looking at, and were unable to read the Latin alphabet let alone understand English. Often they held the passport upside down or back to front, affecting airs of power before eventually asking me what country I was from. Then they laboriously filled in vast, dog-eared ledgers with arbitrary pieces of information that would never be looked at again, asking me to add my profession and signature. My CV through Sudan was colourful. Al Humphreys is on record there as a pigeon fancier, fireman, TV weather man and a pedalo vendor.

There were few distractions apart from the checkpoints, and wondering where the next well would be. The road was hard, hot and boring, three things sure to induce self-pity and question my motivation. When I couldn't bear the heat any more I would cling to the smallest scrap of shade and rest. I lay under a leafless bush amongst dried goat droppings and a snake skeleton. The hard, cracked earth dug into my back. The air was completely still and fiercely hot. Flies danced over my face, and I couldn't summon the energy to waft them away. Never had I known heat like this. The ground was even too hot to sit on for long. I used my sun hat as a pillow and snatched some sleep before the irritating flies persuaded me to ride on. I had to reach Gondar by Saturday.

The philosophy of those days was miles not smiles. I was ahead of schedule but it took a toll on me, and I very nearly cheated. The road was so hot and so dull, with nothing to help pass the time. Only the untrustworthy combination of me and my head. Every movement a trial. I thought I couldn't ride anymore, I knew I couldn't think anymore. Dry, shimmering plains. Scrawny goats. Clattering trucks. Liquid horizon: pale earth meets white sky. Overhead strong blue round massive sun. Sky too big and empty for just one person. Can't ignore that sun. Remorseless sky, so quiet. Empty. Expressionless. Grass huts. People's homes. Life and normality for them. Too hard for me. Truckers' *chai* stops. On and on, and on. Sun too big, too bright, too hot. Headwind brutal. Only 7mph. Damn. Must ride faster. Head pounding protest. Must drink more. Water hot as bath water. Horrible. Can't keep eyes open any more. Need to sleep. Must keep going. Always a little further. Too hot, too hard, too pointless...

Drivers kept stopping their lorries and offering me lifts because riding this fiery road was ridiculous. Maybe I should just have admitted defeat. I had argued this with myself so many times before and had no more urge to keep proving myself to myself. My head was thumping with dehydration. Why not take a lift? I must be mad. No-one would know. (Except me, except me...) Or, sod it, why didn't I just tell everyone I'd taken a lift. I didn't care what people thought anymore. Not that anyone would care. Would skipping a few hundred kilometres make any difference to anything? I hated everyone that drove past, unappreciative of their vehicles. I hated everyone sitting comfortably in England at that moment, unappreciative of their comfort. And I sneered at myself for being too stubborn to end this madness. I began this whole ridiculous affair because I wanted a challenge that I would fail unless I worked extremely hard at it. But now I knew that I could cross mountains or deserts. I knew that I could survive alone in strange countries and situations. I knew that I could handle the grinding routine of the road, the endless foraging for food and water, the daily search for shelter, the constant concerns of safety and dangerous roads, the permits and banks and visas, and the total dependence on the mercy of strangers. I knew that I could do it. I just didn't know whether I wanted to keep doing it. If I knew that I could do it was there any point in actually doing it? So I cried my way through the emptiness. At least it kept my eyeballs cool.

These eternal mental battles and emotional see-sawing helped to pass the time as I watched the kilometres creep beneath my wheels, and the sun moved torturously slowly towards the horizon. The relief when the sun would set and the day would end. Then I would lie back on the sand and unwind. I got into the habit of choosing my favourite moment of each day and reflecting on the lessons that I had learned. I also thought of the thing that I was most looking forward to about the next day. It helped to fall asleep with positive thoughts. It was an amazing privilege to be alone in the desert in Sudan at night. The sunsets burned with such clarity, welcoming me to the cool relief of the dark night and the beautiful stars. I had tested myself that day and I had passed the test. I had not cheated. I started thinking that maybe it wasn't so bad after all… And then my alarm clock would wake me. I would pack and eat in the dark and be back on the road again before the first greying of the dawn. Miles not smiles.

Unlike me, Sudanese hospitality showed no sign of relenting. A group of lorry drivers sitting at a rest stop motioned for me to stop and invited me to share their evening meal. We sat on the ground in the lee of an overloaded lorry. They were bound for Khartoum piled high with scrap metal. By day there may also be as many as forty passengers clinging on top of the piles, hitching a ride between villages. The tyres of the lorry we were next to were bald and gouged, there was only one door and no windscreen. But this was a fine Sudanese lorry because the horn was working, which Ahmed proudly confirmed with a deafening rendition of *Greensleeves* as he departed. No self-respecting Sudanese driver would ever sally forth on a journey without a novelty horn and an excessive number of passengers. Doors and tyres are as unimportant to them as little red breakdown triangles and tins of travel sweets are to us.

The men had weathered, creased faces and magnificent moustaches. Their huge bellies were a testimony to a vigorous exercise routine of eating lots, laughing loudly, driving very fast, and hearty handshakes. Their *galibayahs* were filthy, but before eating they washed their hands meticulously, taking turns to pour water from a jug over each other's hands. We sat on the ground, sharing *fuul* from a communal bowl. Shards of raw red onion added much-needed flavour to the grey mush of beans flaccid below a thick coat of yellow oil. We ripped hunks of bread to scoop up the soft beans, tipping our heads back to help sticky handfuls into our mouths. I joined in happily with the right-handed eating, left-handed backslapping, and full-mouthed laughter. Discussion centred on why farmers in England do not use camels. I struggled to answer. And which tribe was I from? I plumped for 'Yorkshire'. After dinner they climbed back into their cabs, hooted their farewells, shouted "*Maa-salaama!*" and drove on towards Khartoum. And I cycled on down my moonlit road towards Ethiopia.

Cycling at night in the Sudan is like visiting a casino, fun but foolhardy. Potholes were a trivial risk compared to all the vehicles that drive without headlights. Only wimps drive with headlights in the Sudan. Headlights are only used to dazzle on-comers, to express anger that the on-comer had not noticed their pitch black, high speed approach, and to scare the life out of Englishmen on bicycles. As fast as possible I covered the miles and left the road for the safety of my sleeping bag.

The road continued on towards Eritrea but I turned right onto a tiny dirt track towards Ethiopia. The riding was good, a weaving path of warm sand meandering through occasional villages of simple huts, ladies pounding maize in huge mortars, sturdy baobab trees and immaculately swept earth in mosaics of rainbow sweeps. Each village water pump was a colourful and noisy blossom of skirts and plastic containers and shrieks of hilarity and gossip. Water was scarce and long queues wound from the central pump; colourful snakes of plastic buckets and dark jovial women wrapped in swathes of bright fabric. From skinny little girls to sensuously elegant, curvy young women to seriously big mommas, bulks of bum and boob and boisterous noise. Collecting water seemed to be an enjoyed part of the women's daily routine, or at least an accepted burden they made the best of. They had time to themselves, away from their men who were usually busy sitting beneath a shady tree doing bugger all. The women did not hurry and the squeals and roars of belly laughter and gossip suggested that their lives would be infinitely duller with the arrival of the kitchen tap. "How many taps do we have at home?" I asked myself in amazement. Amazement because I had never really appreciated what a ludicrous number we had, but also amazement that my time-passing activities stooped as low as tap counting (other favourite cerebral exercises included pizza planning, devising fantasy football teams and, if time was short, reminiscing on girls successfully wooed)hat was stranger, that it no longer seemed abnormal to me for entire villages to have to queue at a single water pump in the 21st century, or that where I came from everybody had near infinite supplies of water quite literally on tap?

In front of me in the queue a girl was filling an oil drum on a wobbly wooden donkey cart. It was about three days ride from here to the border so I decided to carry 15 litres of water and gamble that I would find additional small settlements on the way to supplement it. Once at the front of the queue I pumped water for a lady while she held her bucket beneath the spout and then she returned the favour for me. I leaned on the long, clanking lever and the water gulped out with each pump. It was hard work. My arm muscles protested, my back ached and the sun was unsympathetic. Throughout Africa my pumping provoked hilarity. I questioned my technique. I questioned my stamina. I didn't know what I was doing wrong. People at home laugh at my dancing. That is understandable. But here I did not understand it – my rhythm was flawless! The comedy though was just the dirty white guy with a bicycle who had ridden unexpectedly into their world. The white people the villagers normally saw raced past in air-conditioned aid agency landcruisers drinking bottled water or cold Pepsi. White people do not queue at village pumps.

I treated myself in a market to *felafel* sandwiches and spicy sauce. As I waited for the small balls spitting and sizzling in the hot oil I looked around the market. It was dirty and very poor, even by Sudanese standards. The haphazard paths between the dusty kiosks were almost too narrow for my bike to pass through. The market was a labyrinth of rickety stalls made from sticks, cardboard and plastic sheets. I watched people buy a single cigarette, half a loaf of bread or a single banana. Arguments erupted over the smallest of coins. It was microeconomics on a miniscule scale. If you sell one of your five bananas you can buy a piece of bread for tonight. There is no planning for tomorrow when every cent you own must be spent to eat today.

I was much taller than everyone pushing past me. People stared at me as always. I could not blame them, I was a filthy and unusual sight. External differences can seem so vast that it becomes easy to believe that people are different. But spend time drinking tea or pumping water or cycling along together and you quickly remember that there are no insurmountable differences at all. Hopes, fears and a sense of humour are among the great constants for all of us.

As I rode out of town some kids threw stones at me. Usually when that happened I would stop and rationally reprimand them or point it out to a nearby adult who would give them a definitive smack round the head, but in this barbarous heat I stopped in my tracks. On the verge of tears, I started screaming abuse at the little boys. This just led to an even larger volley of stones and much laughter. Having stones hurled at you purely because you are different is an unsettling experience, but even so my reaction startled me. What was happening to me? I had had stones thrown at me before. I had had tough stretches of road before. Why was I becoming so edgy and vulnerable? I felt that I was losing control again. I was scaring myself. I tried to tell myself that there are no bad experiences, only lessons. And I imagined what my mates would say if they could see me reduced to tears by a scrawny handful of little eight-year-olds. Ridiculed, amused, and with things back in perspective, I pedalled on.

I was alone in classic African savannah. No more road, just tracks of deep hot sand rolling their way around contours, rocks and bushes. Pitch black birds with crimson breasts and flowing tails shrilled. Small villages of round mud huts with thatched roofs erupted in excitement as I rode through, scattering chickens and pulling crowds of running, whooping, lovely children. This was Africa at last! Old men sat in the sun, wrinkled and wise as elephants, smoking tight cigarettes, playing slow games with white pebbles in the warm dust and putting the world to rights. They watched me pass and raised dignified arms in greeting and moral support. Everyone waved at me and I always returned the gesture. But in the heat this extra effort felt very, very hard. I struggled to do more than limply lift an arm off the handlebar. My fingers remained hooked like a claw and my shoulders stayed hunched. Tough guys may tattoo 'LOVE' and 'HATE' across their knuckles, but I was too hot and tired for such passionate emotions and settled for optimistically writing 'COLD BEER' on my cycling mitts. I hoped that they would have beer in Ethiopia.

I saw a lean-to shelter of coarse grass and two tiny homemade benches serving as a coffee house. I gratefully flopped from my bike into the meagre shade. The few customers shuffled along the bench to make room for me (or perhaps to move away from the sweaty newcomer?). I smiled a greeting. The men jabbered their greetings and shook my hand in welcome. A lady sat on the ground beside a small mound of glowing charcoal. Her hair was covered in a bright red cloth and her broken-toothed smile added years to her age. Around her lay an assortment of small plastic bags. I sniffed and poked them: spices, ground coffee, ginger, sugar. She fanned the coals with a square of cardboard and filled a jug from a big black kettle of stewing coffee. I was given a battered little jug holding enough coffee for about 10 tiny cupfuls. My cup was the size of a shot glass, filled to the brim with sugar and topped up with just a few drops of coffee. I looked at the sweet sludge in my cup with surprise. The customers laughed at me. They showed me that you sipped the syrupy coffee from the top of the cup then topped up the cup from your jug. This meant that every cupful had more coffee and less sugar until the final hit was just pure, bitter coffee. It was black and thick and the cardamom struck my throat. The strong aftertaste glowed around my lips and the caffeine fooled me into thinking how great it would be to just jump back on the good ol' bike and get riding again. So I did. I left this small experience buzzing from both the caffeine and from the reminder that this was why I was on the road, for the innocuous, normal, everyday things like drinking coffee. Because, on the road, nothing is 'normal' or 'everyday'. I was different there, so afloat that I did not even know how to drink coffee properly. When things were not going well, this lack of foundation was frightening, but when things were good, this was the essence of why I chose to travel.

The hills of Ethiopia rose ahead. At yet another roadblock, I asked the policeman whether the dire road conditions improved further ahead. He replied, "No, but don't worry, it will be good in two years' time." Not much use to me, as my teeth rattled inside my skull. The next checkpoint was manned by boy soldiers, dressed in flip-flops and tattered T-shirts, with combs stuck in their hair and grenade launchers hanging from their slender shoulders. Watching them strut around was unsettling as they posed with their lethal hardware, their innocence masked behind a wall of aggression. I checked with one of the kids that I was still on the right path. His geography of far-off places was unusual. He said, "This is road to Ethiopia, then is USA." Further away than just down the road is utterly

Dawn on the Danube

Crossing the Bosporus was a big moment – leaving
Europe behind and heading into the unknown

Camping in the lonely highlands of central Turkey

Christmas Day in Jordan

Map reading, Sudan

Rob came out to ride with me for a couple of
weeks in Ethiopia. My deterioration clearly shows!

Curious children, Ethiopia

Mikumi National Park, Tanzania

Tea plantation, Tanzania

Sharing the road, East Africa

Dugout canoes on Lake Malawi

Basket fishing, Mozambique

Entering the mountains, Lesotho

The end of Africa – a moment to savour,
South Africa

irrelevant to most people on the planet. I wondered which exotic far-off land had made his grenade launcher.

After a couple more days I arrived in Gallabat, the border village. It was a sleepy gathering of huts, unlikely to ever make headline news. Listless dogs wandered with taut ribs and swollen swaying teats. Flies fretted on their eyes and open sores. After the bureaucratic battle I had to fight to get into the Sudan, I was daunted by the prospect of having to do it all again to leave. The big difference though was that I was now so fond of the country, I trusted the people and saw their obsession with irrelevant pieces of paper, arbitrary stamps and meaningless signatures more as an endearing foible than a sinister, secret-police-type pain in the backside. As with everything in Sudan, I was to be pleasantly surprised. Whilst the border formalities took place I sat on the officer's desk in his thatched mud hut with garish floral blankets on the walls. He added a few random details to yet another vast ledger, rummaged around in his pal's desk drawer to find a stamp for my passport, and I was on my way. I was in and out in five minutes. The customs officer was having a nap so I didn't bother with that stage. It seemed a shame to disturb him.

I was reluctant to leave Sudan now, and made excuses to potter around the village for a while. The immigration officer took me to breakfast. He didn't seem concerned about leaving his post unmanned. The chances of an impatient, tutting queue awaiting his return were pretty slim. We ate *felafel* and I wondered nostalgically if it would be my last ever, whilst a comforting fug of incense burned on the coals to keep the flies away. I finished my last mouthful and mustered the resolve to leave.

I remembered arriving in Sudan, uneasy and scared with my head full of preconceptions. I had been convinced that I would be robbed and thought I'd possibly get shot too. But I had now crossed Africa's largest nation and learned so much. Sudan had huge problems, amongst them an awful government, a horrific civil war, hunger, drought and terrible poverty. How could all the devout, decent people I had met be represented by this callous, murderous government? The world takes little interest in African tragedies, and one of the benefits of my journey was my awakening to some of them. Despite their poverty, the Sudanese people I met were happy. They had dignity and self-respect and were content with what little they had. And they had an abundance of friends, family and faith. They were the kindest, most cheerful, hospitable and welcoming people that I had ever met. I pedalled through the village towards Ethiopia with a smile on my face.

ኢትዮጵያ ኤምባሲ
Embassy of Ethiopia
ቆንስላ ክፍል አዲስ አበባ
CONSULAR SECTION. KHARTOUM
VISA NO. 5621-6-94
VISA TYPE TOURIST
GOOD FOR SINGLE ENTRY.
PERMITTED TO STAY IN ETHIOPIA
FOR ONE DAYS/MONTHS FROM
THE DATE OF ENTRY
ALLOWED TO ENTER IN THIRTY
DAYS FROM THE DATE OF ISSUE.
DAYS AND. MAR. 4 19 2002
SEAL SIGN BY

جمهورية السودان
وزارة الداخلية
الإدارة العامة للجوازات والهجرة
والجنسية والبطاقة الشخصية
No 0020744
رقم التأشيرة
تجددت الإقامة حتى Visa Renewed up To
Imm. No.
Date
Sign
التاريخ

A Beautiful Place
to be Born?

The world is a beautiful place to be born into, if you don't mind some people dying all the time, or maybe only starving some of the time, which isn't half so bad, if it isn't you.
Lawrence Ferlinghetti

How can two sides of one village be so different? One hundred metres from Sudan and I had left behind Islam and North Africa and was into the continent's heart. The buildings, people and attitudes all felt different. The red dirt road was busy with pedestrians. Barefoot people and donkeys easily outnumbered the few fume-spewing, rattling vehicles. Women walked shaded beneath golf umbrellas, a strange sight in the African sun. Men bore a stout staff across their shoulders, their hands hooked over it like wings. In Sudan the ladies flowed in colourful loose robes and men with bushy moustaches glided around in white *galibayahs*. In Ethiopia the men wore tight little shorts and tattered T-shirts, repaired many times, with a blanket draped over their willowy shoulders. Many wore Leonardo di Caprio T-shirts, presumably a well-meaning bulk foreign aid donation. Some women's dresses were made from old UN and USAID (US Agency for International Development) grain sacks, others wore bright robes swathed tightly round the body, breasts and neck with their slender arms uncovered. Many were strikingly beautiful. Kids were everywhere, running all around me and laughing and shouting "You! You! You!" as I passed. Most of the children wore rags. A few were naked save for crucifixes or necklaces made from things they had found on the road: keys, nuts and bolts. Some were bald, many had Mohican hairdos. The youngest ones ran screaming from my camera. The older ones demanded to be snapped. Everyone was crazy. I loved it.

I stopped, tired, in the next village, about twenty miles down the track. I was beckoned to a small mud house for coffee. Gratefully I accepted and joined a few men on the end of a low bench outside the door. A crowd huddled around me, staring. Everything felt so different from Sudan. I didn't even know the word for 'hello' in Amharic yet. I smiled and attempted to make a connection. They stared in silence, making no attempt to communicate. The women had crude blue crosses tattooed on their foreheads and symbols on their knuckles and hands. Then one lady handed me a small baby to hold and everybody smiled. She joked that I should take him with me, take him back home. I looked into his enormous shining brown eyes and imagined how different his life would be in Britain. There would certainly be less time to sit and enjoy coffee with friends.

A girl was sitting in the doorway on a spread of grass, grinding freshly roasted coffee beans in a mortar. The coffee was served black in small china cups, person by person, in decreasing order of age. When I returned the baby, gave my thanks for the delicious coffee and left the village a crowd of kids ran around me, laughing and shouting incessantly "YOU! YOU! YOU!" Their novelty was fading, it was baking hot, the road was atrocious. I ignored them. They kept up the mayhem for several miles before I finally bored them into surrender by resolutely ignoring them and not giving them any sweets.

At sunset I hid away from the road in the rocky, bush-strewn mountains. I brewed a cup of tea while I watched monkeys foraging. In each new country it took a while for me to pick up the vibes and to get a feel for how safe I was. I always began very cautiously and built up to my preferred levels of pragmatic recklessness. Minimise risk, cover your back, plan well, then roll the dice. Think carefully and prepare mentally for every potential crisis and then relax and leap in with both feet. I had found a well hidden but rocky campsite behind a small cluster of thorny trees. I did not use my torch. I was tired and could only summon the energy to cook popcorn for dinner and was even concerned that the noise of the popcorn may give away my position. Occasional heavy lorries laboured past up the steep, bumpy track. Later a family walked past babbling loudly to one another. I sat quietly in the dark and listened to the strange sounds of their language, trying to imagine what they may be talking about. I kept still until they passed and then rolled out my sleeping bag on the least rocky patch I could find. "I'm in Ethiopia!" I smiled as I fell through my nerves and excitement into sleep.

Northern Ethiopia took me along a boulder strewn, dusty track climbing steadily up into the craggy mountains. The mountains were the largest I had encountered. Even in bottom gear I could not pedal up some of the gradients and my arms ached as I pushed my way up the hills, my feet struggling for grip in the dust. Battered buses heaved and skidded past me with crunching gears, straining engines and spinning wheels, drowning me in dust. Speakers on the roof pumped jaunty, yearning Ethiopian music, the trumpets, percussion and racing cascades of passionate female vocals. The road was always busy with pedestrians. Ladies carried heavy ceramic water urns roped to their backs or baskets of cow dung on their heads, fuel for cooking. People would bow a greeting as I called out my new-learned hello, "*tadiyas!*" Many men rode heavy black iron bicycles. One almost crashed spectacularly as he tried to bow to me while racing down a gravel track.

I passed through small villages of wood, mud and wattle homes thatched with grass. There was little empty space in Ethiopia. Amongst the clusters of homes would be a tiny shop but the shelves were virtually empty. Stale cardboard-flavoured biscuits, batteries, a rusting tin or two of fish paste, combs, blocks of hard soap and candles sat beneath layers of dust.

My diet here was determined more by availability than by choice. I even ate a packet of sweets that I had hoarded all the way from France.

Crowds of kids gathered everywhere I went, and they stared at me with unabashed astonishment. After several days of being the focus of the freak show I began losing my patience with the children and they started to become a real nuisance. Some children wondered whether I was Chinese, as Chinese road engineers had once worked here. I have never before been mistaken for a Chinaman. Of all the words in the English language, how had they come to know just: 'you' and 'money'? Children, smaller and skinnier than they should have been, tried to pull things off my bike as they ran around me, shouted and jeered, and aggressively demanded money. They pushed me up hills, which was great, but they were always trying to grab things as they ran. I could not allow my bike out of my sight for a moment, and had to look over my shoulder constantly as I rode.

"YOU-YOU-YOU!" they taunted, like a Chinese drip torture.

"Shut up, shut *UP*," I replied, eloquently.

"YOU-YOU-YOU-YOU!" they howled louder.

Adults looked on amused when their children threw stones at me. In one village howls of encouraging laughter followed a boy as he ran beside me trying to jam a stick in my spokes. I sprayed him in the face with my water bottle, feeling proud of my self-restraint. Crowds of gawpers would gather whenever I stopped, staring and making jokes about the *'ferenji'*. I could not hide. Thomas Stevens, the grand-daddy of long distance bike riders, once had occasion to rant in Turkey: 'As I mount, the mob grows fairly wild and riotous with excitement… rushing up behind and giving the bicycle smart pushes forward in their eagerness to see it go faster, and more than one stone comes bounding along the street, wantonly flung by some young savage unable to contain himself.' One hundred and fifty years later in Ethiopia, I knew how he felt. In Ethiopia, Evelyn Waugh wrote: 'Most of the time I thought about how awful the next day would be.'

What struck me most was that the adults had no notion that this was not gracious behaviour. It was so different from Sudan. It is rare in the world to encounter begging in rural areas, except where tourism has gone ahead, but in Ethiopia people demanded cash everywhere I went. A man, sucking on a cigarette, pushed through a crowd in front of me and demanded bread. His look of arrogant, righteous expectation infuriated me and I stuck two fingers up at him. "No, no," he assured me, he only required one loaf from me, not two.

People seemed to have lost the desire, urgency or dignity to sort out their problems themselves. There was a reek of dependence. Ethiopia was the poorest country I had visited and it was hard to imagine that changing. Of course, I was in Ethiopia only a few weeks so it is reckless and naïve of me to generalise, but I could not ignore the atmosphere and attitude that felt distinct and different from elsewhere. The huge input of unconditional aid by Western countries, generalised in local minds as 'white people', seemed to have bred a generation of Ethiopians who wanted to be rich, but didn't want or feel the need to put in the effort for themselves. Why work hard to manage the village water supply when someone will give you bags of grain for nothing?

In Ethiopia I felt like a mobile cash point, and too many people felt that they had a right to be bankrolled by me. I did not feel as though I was regarded as a fellow human being. I could not make contact. I resolved, and continued this around the world, not to give money to individuals, to give only my time and smiles. As the days ground by I longed to be alone, to have some space, but people would even follow to watch me taking a dump.

People everywhere, shouting for money, palms outstretched, laughing at me, jeering. When H Tilman cycled in Africa he said: 'My popularity as a public spectacle was at its height… It sounds merely funny now, but at the time it nearly drove me frantic; possibly my sense of humour was becoming a little blunted now that I had acted the part of a travelling circus for so long.'

It sounds whining and feeble now, but at the time it felt so hard to be permanently the centre of their entertainment. "Money! Money! Money!" How did tiny children know to run at me demanding like that? In the 1970's Ted Simon rode a motorbike round the world and wrote his experiences in his book *Jupiter's Travels*. He said: 'In Ethiopia for once I allowed myself the luxury of a generalization. Two words described them all for me.' And the second one was 'up'.

People were hungry. They had nothing. No money, no work, no hope. So what did they see? A tourist cruising through their lives, taking photos, looking all around in grim fascination, a white boy from the wealthy West passing through their world on a hugely laden, shiny bicycle carrying, no doubt, an incredible wedge of money. This is the worst aspect of being a tourist, that, as Jim Caird wrote, you become 'an ugly, empty thing, a stupid thing, a piece of rubbish pausing here and there to gaze at this and that, and it will never occur to you that the people who inhabit the place in which you have just paused cannot stand you'. It is to their credit that nobody in Ethiopia just kicked the crap out of me and took all my money. Tiny mud homes and large, struggling families; whips cracking the hot air above oxen hauling wooden ploughs across dry, shallow soil; barren land hoed by skinny children; empty shops and empty eyes. I had seen an 1841 lithograph of an Ethiopian ploughing scene. And nothing had changed. Nothing except that early visitor's praise of the Ethiopians' 'scrupulous politeness towards strangers'. The friendly people who had invited me for coffee seemed like an anomaly now.

Overwhelmed by the loneliness of crowds, I stopped riding and sat down on the dirt track. I hid my tears behind my sun- glasses and big hat as the inevitable crowd gathered around, emerging from nowhere to buzz around me, prowling, frolicking, probing, sniggering, provoking. In the midst of these crowds I felt isolated, out of my depth, out of control and alone. My ride felt shallow and indulgent.

Salvation came in the form of Peter, the local teacher. Seeing me amongst the crowd he picked me up and took me to his home, a small mud hut beside the two-room school. I could sleep on his floor, he said in good English. He shooed away the gawping gathering outside his door and I began to unwind. I was keen to talk properly with somebody in Ethiopia, to connect with somebody and to learn about their life. Peter's wife and child lived away in Gondar with her parents, so he only saw them every few weeks. The government had not paid his pittance of a salary for three months yet he was still working. He taught a primary education to the 150 children in each class, one class in the morning, the other in the afternoon, with no textbooks or equipment. In each class the pupils ranged in age from eight to 20. The students only came to school when their family could spare them from ploughing or tending livestock so attendance was rarely continuous. Some had to walk 20 kilometres to school, and then back home afterwards.

Peter talked about his country, the beautiful mountains and greedy politicians. He talked about the vicious famine that brought Ethiopia to the attention of the world in 1984. We gave our pocket money and then turned shocked and embarrassed away from the TV as we tucked into our fish fingers and baked beans. Six months after the Ethiopian government had appealed for international assistance, the unforgettable images of the famine burst on to our television screens and Western governments began to act. Michael Buerk from the BBC spoke of a 'Biblical famine, now, in the 20th century... the closest thing to hell on Earth... death is all around.' That year Europe had a record harvest with huge stockpiles of surplus grain. The Ethiopian government's relief coordination was incompetent and food aid was diverted away from famine victims to feed troops fighting a twenty year civil war. eight million people were at risk and, while the UK public gave £5 million in three days, government response to the Marxist country was still low-key. By December, Bob Geldof's efforts spurred the Western public to donate more than £100m, but the Ethiopian government continued to divert aid supplies to its troops. More than a million people died in that famine. Now I was being hosted by a man the same age as me who had lived through it. I sat beside him on his bed and listened to him tell me about the brother and sister he lost that year.

The hut was lit by stubs of candles and shadows flickered on the dark grass roof above us. The walls were papered with newspaper. The furnishing was a single bed, a wooden chair and school desk, a bowl on the mud floor holding plates, mugs and cutlery and a couple of books on a shelf. I loved the Amharic script in his books, beautiful and unintelligible to me with letters like chicken wishbones. Peter was teaching himself extra mathematics in the evenings to improve his teaching skills. Strips of raw meat hung drying from lines under the roof. Peter saw England as a land of incredible wealth. He had heard that in the West, people even left food outside to feed wild birds. Was this true? He found it hard to accept that there were homeless people and beggars in England. However he absolutely refused to believe me when I told him that most of them were white. "Impossible!" he declared. He could not even imagine a poor white person.

We sat side-by-side and ate *injera* and a spoonful of boiled cabbage with our hands. It was the Easter fasting period in Ethiopia during which no meat is eaten. As large as a family pizza and flat as a pancake, *injera* is served with every meal in Ethiopia. It is a pancake-like bread made from *teff*, a fine millet flour. It serves as bread, tablecloth, plate, cutlery and napkin all in one. 'It is cool, moist and rubbery, less like a crêpe than an old damp bathmat,' wrote Theroux. *Injera* has the complexion of a pasty acne-scarred office worker or the face mask of an alien in a very cheap horror show, the texture of a whoopee cushion and the taste of sour silage. It's an acquired taste.

After dinner we blew out the candles: we both had an early start the next day. I hoped to reach Gondar and Peter had another busy, unpaid day at school. I slept on the floor, reassured that I could find kind people anywhere in the world, and reminded of the steep learning curve that I was travelling on.

The final 10 kilometres up the hill into Gondar was on a paved road, a nice surprise. It even had a white line painted on it. I managed to grab hold of the back of a lorry (most lorries in Ethiopia had thorn bushes dangling off the back to deter this) which dragged me up the last climb, filling my lungs with fumes and stretching my arm.

I sat on the pavement in the centre of Gondar and used my spoon to spread jam on my last piece of bread. I licked my spoon to clean it. A staring man told me in broken English that in his culture it was rude to lick a spoon like that. I replied that in my culture it was rude to throw rocks, shout at people, try to pull things from their bikes and hassle people for money. To my surprise he agreed and sympathised with me. So I wiped my spoon on my trousers instead.

Gondar, the former capital of Ethiopia, was a pretty town, sliding down a hillside of dark forest. A 17th century church, whose ceiling was painted with Ethiopian-looking cherubs, sheltered in the trees above the town. There were quiet cafés in the central plaza, cake shops selling colourful but tasteless sponges and enough people for me to be slightly less conspicuous. There were even one or two other tourists. People seemed busier and had less time to stare at me. A crazy man threw rocks at everyone, not just me, and chased people down the street. There were beggars on every street, shockingly thin or brutally disfigured. A child approached me with no hands: he had picked up a landmine. Blind people prodded their way across the busy streets. A tug at my ankle came from a man with no legs or arms and just tiny hands. In Ethiopia my callow naïvety was being brutally revealed. I was a tree with shallow roots, a boat with a paltry keel and the winds of Ethiopia were merciless.

I found the cheapest hotel in town to wait for Rob's arrival. The 30p room was so small that my bike barely fitted inside, and the unpainted walls were stained with grime and squashed mosquitoes. There was no window, chair, table or light shade. The grey blanket on the sagging grey mattress looked revolting, a bedbug heaven. The ceiling was lower than head height, and the communal pit toilet was across the dirt yard in a bamboo structure the size of a large dog kennel. I had to almost crawl in, squat amongst the used toilet paper (torn strips of newspaper actually) that covered the mud floor, use my torch to assist with aiming at the brown-framed hole and get out again, all within the span of one single breath as I was definitely not going to breathe inside there. Still, if you search out the cheapest hovel in town what do you expect?

While I was waiting for Rob, I wanted to try *tej*. *Tej* is Ethiopian mead. My impressions of a buzzing bee, a man glugging liquid, and a man rolling across the decks of joyful inebriation got me pointed in the right direction, and I found an unmarked *tej* bar. *Tej* looks like orange juice and is served in glass flasks, called *berele*, resembling those used in chemistry experiments. It tastes like sharp, fizzy honey. The bar was dark, with wood shavings on the floor. Apricot light shafted through gaps in the walls and dust motes twirled in the beams. Old men wrapped in white robes leaned on their sticks and smoked hard. The air droned with idle conversation. Nobody minded that I was in their bar, and it felt wonderful to be ignored.

That night the crazy old bat running the hovel locked me into my room, and for the first time on the trip I fell ill. I could not get out of the room. Fortunately there was a green plastic bowl in the room. It filled ever higher with my vomit. *Tej* tastes better going down than coming back up. After each retching heave I looked anxiously to see how much space remained in the bowl, and the night dragged endlessly. I crossed my legs and fought the gripping stomach cramps: the bowl was too full to surrender to that need! I flew from the room as soon as the bolt was drawn back from my door at sunrise. I felt frail but much better as I emerged gasping for breath from the horrible toilet.

I sat in the plaza, read a book and wrote in my diary while I waited for Rob. I knew that I wouldn't need to make any effort to rendezvous, word would arrive through an unusual intelligence network of 10-year-old boys. Gondar had a fledgling tourist market, just enough to keep a cluster of young boys busy making life easier for the handful of tourists, organising, advising, guiding, running errands, shooing away other touts.

At first they got on my nerves, pestering me all the time, but one boy, by the name of Million, impressed me. His English was fantastic, his father was a teacher, he had procured a small suit from somewhere, he was bright and polite, and he knew everything. I promised him I'd buy him a cake if he brought Rob to me. The next morning Rob landed at the small local airport from Addis and took a taxi into Gondar. Conspicuously new to Ethiopia (clean clothes, smiling at the "you, you, you"-ing kids), Million found him in a flash. Rob wondered who this precocious chap was, but his description of me convinced Rob that Million did know me. I would never have bought the little bugger his Coke and cake if I had known that I was described as "...very dirty and staying in the cheapest hotel that is not for tourists".

It was so good to see Rob again. Friends since school, we were at Edinburgh University together and he was currently at Oxford taking the same teaching degree that I had done had shared many adventures, and I blamed Rob for everything that I was doing now. During a very tedious Statistics lecture back in the first year at University I had been woken by Rob leaning forward and passing a note down to me, along the lines of, "Can you travel Karakorams in June?" That summer we cycled the Karakoram Highway from Pakistan over the mountains to China and I was hooked.

Now we laughed and joked and my illness was fast forgotten as we filled each other in on our respective adventures of the last six months. Rob had brought along the new bike to replace Rita that I had organised by email whilst in Khartoum and also a bag of goodies including a Cadbury's Crème Egg for Easter, English newspapers and a letter from Sarah. I decided to save that for later. It was lovely to see Rob, but it also brought instability back into my life with news from home racing through my thoughts once again.

The streets of Gondar were packed, a bike race had been organised in celebration of National Tuberculosis Day. There was one race for motorbikes and one for bicycles. The cyclists rode old shopping bikes but had squeezed into the tightest clothes possible to try to look like professional riders. One man was wearing football boots, another had squeezed into what could only have been his wife's tights. The crowd was boisterous and only a narrow strip of road remained clear between the cheering masses. There were only three contestants in the motorbike race but they were not deterred, and it was a noisy battle, raucously egged on to ever more reckless cornering by the howling supporters.

The morning after the race we cycled out of town early, Rob riding my new bike from Specialized, and I on Rita. I was happy to leave my hovel, but the bedbugs were sad to see me go. Venus gleamed in the East, the mountain air was fresh and the sun had not quite risen as we freewheeled down the hillside in the yellow dawn light. Watching Rob ride ahead, the contrast amused me. His clothes were clean and intact, his bike swooshed silently, and he was whizzing along with enthusiasm. The sight of him highlighted my own physical and mental state. I tried to see Ethiopia through his eyes: yesterday he had been in London and now it was huts and men with spears and hunger and poverty and scorching heat and rutted roads. By coming so gradually to Africa from England – mile by mile, day by day, town by town – everything seemed quite normal to me. I needed to remind myself not to lose my wonder.

A steep, steep climb and our clothes darkened, soaked with sweat. At the top we lay in the shade and looked down to the shining disc of Lake Tana on the horizon, still a few days ride ahead. A pick-up truck full of soldiers swept by in a great balloon of dust. Casually hefting big guns by the armful, and looking tough in their fake RayBan shades, they had all shoved wads of pink toilet paper up their noses against the dust.

Even though we were riding in a pair, the children still mobbed us laughing, shouting, chasing, pulling our bikes, chucking stones. Village after village this went on and I would rant to Rob about how annoying they were. Rob was still in the phase of travelling where everything was exotic, so I felt like a real grumpy old sod. It seemed to me though that I got pelted by more stones than Rob did because he always rode ahead of me and so, after him, the children had time to prepare for my arrival. I raced ahead of Rob as we approached the next village and put my theory to the test. For additional spice I shouted and snarled at every kid that chased me. After the village I paused to admire my handiwork. Rob is the calmest, most decent person I know, so I was delighted to hear his shouts and swearing back in the village. If Rob was losing his temper then things must be maddening.

I challenged myself not to get mad at the kids. I failed. Exasperated, I told one lot, "Sudan children good, Ethiopia children bad." They found this hilarious and chased me down the road shouting, "Ethiopia bad! Ethiopia bad!" Later when we camped behind a small hill and a small group of children discovered us, they just stared silently from a few metres away. They were shy, quiet and curious and I tried to reassure them with a smile. Everything we did or said seemed to them to be mesmerising. They could not have been more transfixed if we had flapped our arms and flown away. Rob offered them tea but they giggled and squirmed and declined. Our arrival was such an exciting surprise that they did not know what to make of us. I wished that I was not hindered by language barriers in Ethiopia more than ever. The children had no TV, games, books, homework or computers to pass the time so they were content instead to gawp at us for a couple of hours. It was no less mindless than television, I suppose. Eventually, as night fell, the children melted away homewards. How I wish I could have understood their excited chatter as they ran across the fields towards their home.

Rob cooked dinner, I pointed out the constellations I had learned over the last months and he told me of his classroom traumas back in Oxford. We were only about 30 kilometres from Lake Tana, and hoped to reach the lake just after breakfast. I looked forward to days off with the passion of an office worker. We had been climbing solidly for a few days and were now high in a land of rolling grassland and clusters of trees. The dusty road had been tough going, our lips were cracked and sore.

Lake Tana was somewhere on our right, somewhere between us and where the sun had set. Ibises flew overhead, their long bills reaching towards Lake Tana for the night, urging themselves onward with their noisy chorus of "Haa-haahaa-haa". We rolled out our sleeping bags on the hard, broken earth.

The hills of Ethiopia were tough; straight, hard pulls or long winding hairpins up out of the parched lands into dark, fragrant forests as green as home. Only three or four gears still worked on my bike and I often had to get off and push. The downhills were not much of a consolation as I nursed my battered bike with her feeble brakes down the rough gravel. Rob had no such worries though on my nice new bike and he descended like a wildman past columns of sheer rock jutting hundreds of feet up into the sky. Nearby Mount Wehni, a formidable black thumb of rock, was once a cliff-top prison for princes who were heirs to the Emperor until their time came to rule. Keeping the princes imprisoned up there protected the Emperor from potential coups. Rob raced on, gear bouncing from his bike as he disappeared towards the horizon in rolling balloons of dust. He was so much faster than me that when I eventually caught him up, after gathering up all his spilled possessions, he was lying under a tree and reading. "Hello," he said, looking up absent-mindedly from the pages, clearly wondering what had taken me so long.

Rob cheered as we rode into Bahir Dar down wide boulevards of palm trees and jacaranda to the pretty lakeshore. Lake Tana, the largest lake in Ethiopia, is the source of the Blue Nile so it was a big landmark for me. I had ridden the longest river. From here the Nile slides out on its long journey, mirror smooth and gentle, accelerating and exploding, thundering over the massive Blue Nile Falls in a smoking cloud of rainbow- ringed rage, unstoppable and endless, churning until the torrent calms to a firm glide past Abu Simbel glowing bronze, silent in the rising sun, then around the peaceful islands and graceful sails of the feluccas at Aswan, and finally back towards the Mediterranean and the dirty clamour of Cairo. I leapt into the lake in all my clothes to give them a bit of a swill. Lake Tana was rife with bilharzia, but I had already decided to ignore that. So many lovely African swimming spots have bilharzia and I preferred, however foolishly, to let my liver host a few worms rather than miss the rare swimming opportunities. There were crocodiles in the lake too, so I tried to always keep on the shore side of the more meaty and appetising Rob. I could not swim faster than a crocodile but perhaps I could swim faster than Rob. We pitched the tent on the shore amongst trees and bushes of extravagant yellow and red blossom. Above us pelicans and hornbills wheeled, cormorants swooped, and large birds of prey circled the heights. It was truly beautiful and there was not a child in sight. The silence hung in tangible enormity around me, the stillness and peace like a vast protective shield.

On April Fool's morning, we locked the bikes in a hotel and hitch-hiked towards the village of Lalibela. High on a lofty escarpment in the central highlands, 13th century monolithic cave churches, hewn down into the bedrock, stand proudly as one of the many Eighth Wonders of the World. It took two days and many different bouncy rides to get there, clinging to the roof of lorries grinding up through the mountains, sitting in the back of crowded pick-ups, arriving late in dark villages and sleeping in basic roadhouses. In one village we walked into the innocuous sounding 'Bingo Club Bar' but beat a hasty retreat when we saw that the only occupants were a cluster of bored prostitutes. The bingo call of 'Two fat ladies!' would have had unpleasant consequences in that village brothel. Waiting in a market for an onward bus, a man was selling sheep's wool in bundles equal to the weight of an old car battery. An old woman sold sandals made from tyres and a honey seller blew on a smouldering pile of charcoal to deter the bees with the smoke. We bought some honey and the man psyched himself up, washing his hands vigorously and rubbing them quickly together before plunging his right hand deep into his sticky bucket, thick with bees, and scooping out a handful of honey which he scraped into a jar for us. The market was on a spur of a hill jutting out into the sky. Brown land fell away below us and down, down to the faint valley floor far below.

Across the valley, high above us were crisp blue outlines of the mountains beneath the clear sky studded with little puffs of cloud. Samuel Johnson described the Giant's Causeway as 'worth seeing, but not worth going to see'. The churches of Lalibela were certainly worth seeing, but they were even more worth going to see.

Back at Lake Tana I loaded up 'Rita I' for the last time, feeling a little guilty at how eager I was to trade her in for the younger, sexier 'Rita II'. Such are men. 'Rita II' was exactly the same as Number 1, a direct swap from Specialized, a mid-range steel mountain bike, with tyres and racks for long-distance riding. The major plus point was the fully-functioning brakes, gears and wheels. Things I had come to think of as luxurious. Rob and I had only a few more days together before he had to go back to work, to walk into his classroom clean-shaven, smart and responsible, and ask his pupils whether they had had a nice holiday. His flight was from Addis Ababa, and it was a long ride. We had no time to spare, so reluctantly we left the warm waters of Lake Tana for the road, pedalling fast south out of Bahir Dar.

Ethiopia is cut roughly in two by the 250 mile gorge of the looping Blue Nile, a spectacular mile-deep canyon of similar proportions to the Grand Canyon. We had to cross it. The road wound and folded down into the bowels of the gorge, far warmer than up on the lip, crossed the river, and then the climb began up the other side. I felt as though I was trapped in an Escher lithograph as the hairpins wound onwards and upwards. Up and up we climbed. We continued pushing the bikes up the gorge for three hours after dark, drank from a muddy trickle beside the road and lay down to sleep, too tired to bother hiding. Sometime later we were woken by a truck. It stopped close to us and we heard the door being thrown open. We were in the full glare of the headlights. The driver approached us in the beams. His gun was silhouetted on his shoulder. Reaching us he stopped, looked at us, turned and then walked back to the truck. His curiosity satisfied, he drove on, never saying a word. I was very relieved to see him go, whoever he was.

We had been repeatedly warned about the dangers of bandits on the roads after dark. Sunrise saw us already on the move again, pushing our bikes up to the lip of the enormous canyon.

Ethiopia grew greener and more fertile down in the south, bursting with fecundity. I felt that only corruption, mismanagement and poor infrastructure could leave people starving and malnourished there. I was in raptures at the sights, sounds and smells that accompany vegetation. It had been a long ride through the arid lands of Turkey, the Middle East and Sudan. I crushed some grass in my hand and inhaled the wonderful fresh aroma: the smell of home! TE Lawrence also raved about the freshness of England from the arid sterility of the desert: 'Was it merely that long ago we had seen fresh grass growing in the spring?'

Ethiopia is unique in many ways; looks, culture, religion, language, food, drink, music. Different from Muslim North Africa, different from Bantu southern Africa, Ethiopia more or less escaped the European Scramble for Africa. Ethiopia has its own calendar, roughly seven years behind the Gregorian. When we were in Ethiopia it was still 1994. The time was told differently too; one o'clock means one hour after sunrise. The months are also out of sync with ours which means, as Rob pointed out, that the song *'Do they know it's Christmas time at all?'* is probably quite right that they did not.

We cut it very fine for Rob to make his flight and we were having to pedal like mad to make it on time, rushing past hobbled donkeys and the carcasses of derelict tanks littering the highway to the capital. We longed for tarmac. The road jarred our bones and bikes, drained our strength and slowed us dramatically. It was a huge relief and surprise then when we suddenly purred onto a paved road, funded by the EU, that whisked us quickly on towards Addis. The mix of rusting vehicles, inexperienced drivers, donkeys and pedestrians on the tarmac was terrifying though. Combined with a smooth, high speed road, the traffic was a recipe for slaughter.

On our final night together we were preparing dinner in the tent when some vehicles stopped on the road, which was a way off, and we heard people get out and start walking towards us. We sat still in the darkness. The sound of a rifle bolt being snapped back froze my blood and for some reason I started whispering frantically at Rob, "Quick, quick: keep chopping the avocado! Look innocent!" Rob humoured me and chopped furiously. Crunching through the dry grass came six silhouettes of approaching men. I offered a tentative greeting and, as they approached the tent, the men lowered their guns. The men were road workers and thankfully they were even more relieved than we were once we had seen each other properly. They had thought that we were bandits setting up an ambush on the road. We offered them some avocado ("Yes, in our country we always chop it very finely"), they wished us a good journey and returned to their vehicle. Beneath an extraordinary electric storm we celebrated our ride with the miniature Christmas pudding that I had saved since Jordan for a special occasion.

Up a big hill we had been hanging on to a truck, and our first view of Addis Ababa came as soon as we let go. Cresting the hill, it spread low in the valley before us. From wide central avenues and tower blocks the city spread out to the surrounding hills, tiny huts blurred in the still morning air by smoke from countless cooking fires. We toasted our arrival in the city with St. George's beer, on tap for 10p. The bar insisted that you bought your beer two at a time which seemed like a clever sales tactic. We clinked our four glasses in a toast and Rob, filthy, scrawny and absolutely exhausted, looked as though he had been immersed in the madness of Ethiopia. Back home it would take him weeks to recover, both physically and mentally: from the hard riding, the tough moral and aid issues, and from the gauntlet of passing among the Ethiopian people. I still had half of Ethiopia to cross. I couldn't wait to reach Kenya.

I was kindly invited for a drink at the Sheraton Hotel in Addis Ababa by some English friends of friends. The luxury of one of Africa's most opulent hotels was staggering, and my memories of that evening now are uncomfortable. I cannot deny enjoying the cold beer, the oil paintings, the sofas, or the dazzling toilets which would have been nicer to sleep in than most of the homes I had seen in Ethiopia. The massive, illuminated water fountains that danced in time to the strains of the Ode to Joy and Rule Britannia. But on the other side of the high security fence were rusty slums and people who had to queue to collect unclean water in buckets. The hotel boasted some of the 'largest and most prestigious banqueting facilities in Africa', 'elegant guestrooms' and an 'extraordinary selection of fine restaurants'. Heated swimming pools played underwater music. It was promoted as being ideal for foreigners who were in Addis with the UN or the NGO aid agencies. It was obscene. In my experience there had been a direct correlation riding through Ethiopia between the villages that had noticeboards announcing that this village had been kindly helped by such-and-such a charity, and the villages where I was treated rudely. Now, on top of that, to sit in such expensive luxury designed for the very people who were supposed to be helping poor Ethiopians, the Mrs. Jellybys and Mr. Quayles, left me feeling deeply uneasy. My time in Ethiopia left me confused about the complicated issues involved in foreign aid.

My confusion continues today – the journey over – sitting in Starbucks in central London waiting for a meeting. I am the only scruffy person. All around me suits are staring at sleek laptops and pearls and pashminas discuss documents. A woman sips from a mug as big as her head and makes a correction on her page. A yuppie toys with a brownie as he listens on his mobile phone. Big decisions take place. Choose your coffee, Americano, Mocha, Macchiato. Choose the size. Choose extra espresso shots. Choose syrups, soy milk, whipped cream. Oh, and a muffin too please. On the wall are stylish photographs of coffee beans, lush plantations, gushing water pumps, smiling workers and a lovely-looking grass hut which I recognised immediately as being from southern Ethiopia. As I sipped my fairtrade coffee and read the captions about how Starbucks is helping communities in Ethiopia I thought of the reality of that idyllic hut beneath a bright blue sky, so far from the rush and rain of London. I thought of the clouds of flies, the foul smoke of cooking fires, the struggle for food, the brutally hard work of survival for that over-stretched family. A confusion of caffeine and Foo Fighters thumping in my headphones is not conducive to calm, mellow reflection. Suddenly I want to shout with rage, a frustrated, impotent anger at the injustice of it all. I do not want to shriek at the uncaring, affluent customers around me; after all, it is my own swanky little iPod and expensive coffee that has got me all worked up. Nor am I furious at the enormous corporation milking their slender social responsibility activities to boost their trendy image – a £50,000 donation to improve the water supply in Ethiopia may be pennies for Starbucks, but at least they do something. Whether that something is to help or whether it is to patronise and create dependence is debate for a few espressos later. What infuriates me is the unfairness. I am looking back now from the other side of the fence. I have got out. I could always get out. Get out whenever I wanted. I can hop back and forth as it suits me. I could sleep in my bed at home tonight, and one of Starbucks' quaint, charming, disease-ridden, verminous grass huts tomorrow. I have the choice. An accident of birth has made it all so easy for me, so hard for them. What can I do? What must I do? What can they do? What must they do? Does drinking fairtrade coffee achieve anything more than giving me a buzz to rant and a brief salve to my conscience? My coffee costs more than a coffee picker's daily income. What is fair about that?

Back in Addis I visited the embassies of Rwanda and Angola to investigate the feasibility of acquiring visas. The Angolans refused me, and I only wanted to go to Rwanda if I could get through to the Democratic Republic of Congo. I could not find a DRC Embassy in Addis so I postponed my enquiries until Nairobi.

The *Cycle to the Summit* team were in Addis. I knew that the Kenyan police would not allow me to ride the first stretch of Kenya alone because of marauding gangs of Somali bandits, but I hoped that perhaps they would treat a group of five more leniently. I decided then to ride with them to the border. The south of Ethiopia promised to be a beautiful ride and we whizzed out of Addis on a smooth paved road past massive charity landcruisers with plenty of empty seats, laden pedestrians trying in vain to hitch rides, a dead hyena, singing bee-eater birds with bright breasts and sharp beaks, old priests sitting beneath umbrellas and collecting alms and a young boy who was trying to sell a single egg to the passing traffic. Boys standing by the road sold watermelons, bananas, avocados, pineapples, papaya and sugarcane and we gorged as we cycled. The fruit was totally localised – you could never buy a papaya in a pineapple village.

The villages of small, round homes with conical thatched roofs looked attractive amongst the lush green trees, hills and coffee plantations. Smoke from cooking fires seeped through the grass roofs. Most of the people seemed generally more polite and amiable than the northern folk. Some days it felt like being in the London marathon, so enthusiastic was the cheering and clapping in every village we passed through. Villages smelled pungently of sweat, smoke and spicy food. The women also glossed their hair with clarified butter which reeked. Children's teeth were brown and stained, apparently from the local water, although I cannot imagine that the endless sugarcane sticks helped much.

The enormous crowds of staring people did not relent and outside one café we counted 200 people gawping at us. We were not doing anything remotely interesting: we were all fully clothed. The owner of the café came to our rescue, hurling buckets of water over the crowd and wielding a stick to drive them away. One man emerged from the crowd to speak to us. "I love England people," he said. That made a nice change from the usual opener of "Give me money." But he continued, "I love England people: they promise and they give you something." I left Toby to deal with him and turned to chat with Ruth.

Almost as annoying as the staring crowds were the flies. I constantly waved one hand over my food when I ate to try to keep them away. The children were less fussy than me and barely flinched as flies walked across their faces, supping from cold sores and runny noses. Everyone's backs were covered with them. I thought of the ancient Pharaohs who used to have servants standing in the corner of the room covered in milk especially to draw the flies away from them.

Qat has been popular around the Horn of Africa for centuries, and I was interested to try this legal drug. Toby and I chewed some one day as we rode, stuffing a wad of the crispy leaves into our cheeks until they softened to a soggy pulp. I had read of effects similar to smoking joints after a few espressos but it just tasted nasty and didn't seem to have much effect. On a long straight we managed to grab hold of the back of one of the few lorries that was not protected with branches of thorns by swerving out in front of it so that it was forced to brake and slow down. We could then grab hold of the back as it passed. We sped ahead of the others gleefully, chewing on our qat all the while. All was going wonderfully until Toby leaned round the back of the lorry to have a look at the road ahead and crashed smack into a roadside wheelbarrow of oranges. It was a spectacular collision. Fortunately nobody was hurt. Toby, the orange salesman and I howled with laughter as we dashed around gathering up the strewn fruit. It was fabulous to laugh and joke with an Ethiopian as I hated the siege mentality of them-versus-me that had welled up in me and festered in recent weeks. Being fairly certain that I spotted a dog copulating with an unconcerned sheep later that afternoon made me question whether perhaps the *qat* was actually stronger than I had assumed. We later gave away our bunch of *qat*, the size of a decent bunch of flowers, to a grateful, and already stoned, old man.

Beyond the beautiful birdlife, the hornbills, pelicans and storks of Lake Awassa, was the village of Shashemene where devoted Rastafarians from round the world have gathered to live and worship on land donated by the Emperor Haile Selassie, formerly known as Ras Tafari, to help Rastafarians return to the motherland. One white Canadian Rasta, clearly devoted in his worship of ganja, was a source of much entertainment to the village's children who chased his stoned and stumbling dreadlocks down the street, shouting over and over, "Haile Selassie is dead!" It made a change from "You! You! You!" I suppose.

Dawns were thickly misted until the sun rose high and the mist faded away into the trees. At the top of a mountain the shadow of a soaring vulture circled us as we rode. We met a man called Alemayo wearing a long red scarf and carrying a *krar*, an instrument similar to a lyre. We danced to his jazzy, funky impromptu performance, five whites shaking our asses as best we could on a quiet hilltop road. We were put in our place by the fabulous pulsating, wiggling rhythm of the local children who inevitably gathered. They laughed at us, and showed us how to dance.

The land was a deep rich red, scattered with tall termite mounds and acacias. The villages were increasingly chilled out and peaceful, the locals independent and busy with their own lives. It was lovely riding. Suddenly in one village scores of children chased us, shouting a whole Christmas list of demands, "Give me money!" "Give me pen!" "Give me sweets!" "Give me bicycle!" (the last chap was *very* optimistic!) and trying to pull things off our bikes. At the end of the village was a huge banner saying, "This village helped by so-and-so charity." I had seen enough.

On the final afternoon a battering storm exploded out of a dark sky, the rain fizzing on the road, bouncing and rushing in spontaneous red torrents. We rode jubilant, soaked, shouting, laughing and marvelling at the ferocious power of the natural world, singing at the top of our voices. Racing on out of the back of the storm we continued to pedal on in the sunshine as fast as we could. The border was just a few hours away. We rode faster and faster. Our clothes dried quickly, the road steamed and the world smelt so clean and fresh. I felt as though I was going to explode with life. Ethiopia. What a place. Fascinating. Infuriating. Proud. Grovelling. Distinctive. Desperate. Dramatic...

As the Kenya border approached I was delighted to be getting out of Ethiopia. I have never sworn at so many people in one country (thank goodness my words were not understood, though presumably the sentiment often was). Yet I also knew that the country had been one of the most important of my journey. Ethiopia had opened my eyes to issues of aid and poverty and exposed me to questions I had never before been forced to address. Above all, Ethiopia had opened my eyes wider to myself. I reflected, with enormous shame, of how in one unbearably obnoxious village I had had the urge to take out some money and burn it in front of everybody. What kind of a sick thought was that? How had my mind been driven to that? Ethiopia was an extraordinary place that I had not been strong enough to deal with. I used to think that I had all the answers. Now, 7,500 miles from home, I realised that I only had questions.

KVP13W/H

EXIT KENYA
19.5.2002
NAMANGA

KENYA
★ AENV ★
IMMIGRATION OFFICER
14 APR 2002
MOYALE

SEEN AT THE PASSPORT
CONTACT OFFICE
KENYA

GOOD FOR SINGLE JOURNEY
TO ___ KENYA
WITHIN THREE MONTHS OF
DATE HEREOF, IF PASSPORT
REMAINS VALID
HOLIDAY

SIGNED ___
14-04-02

DR B720282
US #50

Golden Joys

I speak of Africa and golden joys.
William Shakespeare (Henry IV)

If generalisations have any substance at all, it is possible to break the world down into regions that are broadly similar. They may be similar in language, or looks, or culture, religion, history, personality, diet, mindset or way of life. Once I started to understand how a region worked my life became far simpler. I could develop routines that simplified my days, spending less time working out whether I needed to haggle for bananas or if the price was fixed, learn where were the easy places to stop and ask for water, find people I could entrust with my bike while I shopped in markets, cheap places to buy food, safe places to seek shelter at night. I would get a feel for how safe the drivers generally were; how hard I needed to concentrate on the traffic. I understood whether people were generally honest, or generally liable to rip me off. Everything became easier once I got the hang of a region. I had ridden through Western Europe, Eastern Europe, the Middle East, North Africa and Ethiopia (which I am unable to bracket with anywhere else I have ridden!), and now I entered sub-Saharan Africa. There were many similarities from here down to Cape Town. Indeed, if you say 'Africa' to somebody, the instant images that they will conjure are probably images of the Africa that I rode from Kenya to the Cape. Animals, AIDS, savannah, sunsets, Maasai, Zulu...

The Middle East and Sudan had felt as though they would hold huge difficulties, yet they turned out well. Ethiopia had been harder than I expected, but I had never worried about east and southern Africa and I felt myself relax more than I had in months. Many more people could speak English in this region and I had also spent time before in southern Africa. I knew what to expect. I felt that I already knew much of what I needed to help get me through.

To my dismay though, the Kenyan border police forbade even our large group from travelling without an armed guard. Five bicycle pumps made better self-defence weapons than just one, but the police would not budge loaded our bikes onto a truck with disgust. This was becoming too regular for my liking. At the Isiolo checkpoint, past the alleged wild gangs of marauding Somali bandits, the armed convoy broke up and I could ride on alone towards Nairobi.

I was looking for a fresh start in Kenya, a new era of happiness, enquiry and adventure, to rebuild after Ethiopia my wanderlust and belief in the decentness and warmth of Africa. Kenya's reputation did not suggest that this was particularly likely. Nairobi, the capital, is known as Nai-robbery, and as I rode through Nanyuki, children in English football shirts fired the finger at me and shouted, "Get out, *mzungu* (white man)!" with cockney accents. The British Army trains at Nanyuki and British culture seemed to have rubbed effortlessly from the squaddies onto the locals.

Some people in the countryside – Samburu, Rendille, Boran and Turkana – wore European clothes and fake Manchester United shirts abounded. I was saddened to see this, not because their traditions were being ousted by western nylon, but because of their terrible choice of football club. I felt a real thrill though at the Samburu people I met who were dressed in their traditional red check cloth, wearing countless loops of bead necklaces and elaborate beaded earrings. Stupidly, I felt excited that these were real people, not just images on the

TV, real humans, fleshed out in solid skin, muscle and bone. Lungs sucking and puffing air, hearts thumping and coursing blood, haemoglobin clutching oxygen and surging through miles of tangled capillary. People with tales of life and charged with hopes and worry. Coughs, itches, aches, dreams. Men and women. Pasts and futures. The feel of their warm, calloused hands, the sounds of their speech, the sweet smell of sweat and cooking fires. On the road my senses filled out the photographs and prose of all the books and magazines which in themselves had fired me to travel, propelled me out of England's greyness to see for myself whether people like the Samburu really did exist in wonderful, singing, dancing, three dimensional full colour.

The bleached skies, the shiny dark torsos, the whirring flight of heavy beetles, the balance of a spear I held and pretended to take aim… It was all so distant from my training grounds sitting hunched over a book on rocking trains, rattling and squeaking, my reading interrupted by: "All tickets, please!" and "We are sorry to announce the delay of…" and "Hello, darling, I'm just calling to say that my train has been delayed again." Looking dully out of rain-streaked windows at commuter pay-and-display car parks dotted with puddles and fenced with chainlink tangled by brown brambles and rubbish, at muddy football pitches and industrial parks, handkerchief gardens behind terraced homes and lead-grey skies, rough territorial fencing between allotment plots squeezed between railway and roads jammed to a stop with traffic, pavements black with trodden leaves, piles of burst bin liners dropped from bridges, identical cul-de-sacs individualised by their satellite dishes, mini-roundabouts, sallow strip lights illuminating hunched shoulders in offices noosed with Disney ties… To read there of the semi-nomadic Samburu, or of Kyrgyz shepherds tending herds on high alpine pastures was a thrilling escape from my normality, and yet it never quite felt real. There was always a sliver of my brain that could not quite equate it all with normal people like me. I needed to see for myself. I needed to shake their hand.

Africa had much more in store for me. The Swahili word 'safari' means 'journey' and my own safari still had far to go as I talked and laughed with people so splendidly uncrushed by British Rail. Relaxed men leaning on spears, bare-breasted women swathed in bands of beads with close-cropped hair, and large hoops in their ear lobes. I wonder whether they found a skinny white guy arriving on a bike from the rainy lands of the north to be as striking.

I was cycling on the left-hand side of the road for the first time since Dover after a disorganised changing-over-to-driving- on-the-other-side-of-the-road area at the Ethiopia-Kenya border. Scrubland bloomed into rolling green fields, hedgerows, sheep, cloudy skies and red phone boxes. I was amongst signs in English, tourist touts hassling you to buy carvings of animals, white people, British soldiers, decent cars, and even a cashpoint. My senses were racing at so much novelty. The main street in Nanyuki looked like a throwback to the 1950's: no chain stores, no flashy advertising, just a row of individually owned stores fronted with wooden verandas like the Wild West, yet still so prosperous compared with Ethiopia. Grocers, hardware shops, stationers, liquor stores. I enjoyed being able to read shop signs again: 'We sell sugar, rice, cement' and, oddly, 'Dust for sale'. Schools proclaimed cheery choruses of catchy mixed-metaphor slogans: 'Through discipline, hard work and diligence, the little angels of today will grow into the new trees of the world.' My favourite early impression of Kenya were the cafés where I discovered plates of sausage and chips and mugs of sweet, milky tea as an alternative to *ugali*, the ground maize staple of sub-Saharan Africa that looked like mashed potato and tasted of nothing. Sausage and chips became my staple road food in Kenya. What a great country! I hadn't had a sausage in months. Not a sausage.

At dawn I rode across the equator and into the southern hemisphere. The day was slowly pinking above the stark and rugged Mount Kenya. I paused at the World War II cemetery for

Allied soldiers at Nyeri, stunned that the Europeans' madness had spread as far as these tropical mountain flanks.

Past the flame trees of Thika I rode up a winding country lane through bushy coffee plantations past stunning gabled homes to a friend's house. Justin had been at university with me and he had arranged for me to visit his grandparents as he was still living in the UK. Their home reminded me of the opening words of Karen Blixen's *Out of Africa*: 'I had a farm in Africa, at the foot of the Ngong Hills. The equator runs across these highlands, a hundred miles to the North, and the farm lay at an altitude of over 6,000 feet. In the daytime you felt that you had got high up, near to the sun, but the early mornings and evenings were limpid and restful, and the nights were cold. In the Highlands you woke up in the morning and thought: Here I am, where I ought to be, therefore here I belong.'

Justin's family was my first experience of a different side to life in Africa, the white tribes of Africa, wealthy and influential groups in the history of the continent. Justin's friendly grandparents, dressed in khaki shorts with matching pulled-up socks, greeted me warmly with the clipped accent of white Africans. I walked in amazement across the wide lawns into the enormous house. Polished wooden floors reflected softly the light from driftwood lamps. Sweeping open-plan rooms walled with bookshelves, comfortable sofas that I could barely wait to loaf on, African ebony art carvings framing the fireplace. It was a stunning home. Had I really been laughing with spear-bearing herders that morning? And, more importantly, was that bacon I could smell from the kitchen?

The next day I was alone in the house. I snuggled onto one of the sofas and picked up a book called It's not about the bike by a cyclist called Lance Armstrong. I knew nothing about him, nor about the Tour de France, come to that. I read the book in a single sitting. A man who has it all is almost killed by cancer. He recovers to not only compete in, but to actually win the Tour de France, the toughest bike race on Earth. It was a staggering story; too improbable for fiction and a red-hot cattle prod for anyone thinking their hurdles were high or their days hard.

It was a lesson in choosing from our two options: 'to give up or to fight like hell.' I read the book several more times during my journey, bought it often as a present for people and became a committed Lance groupie. He impressed me, shamed me and inspired me often along the road. 'Lives of great men all remind us we can make our lives sublime, and departing, leave behind us footprints on the sands of time.'

In Kenya I began to feel, for the first time, that I was getting closer to breaking the magnetic field of England, the luring pull back towards all that I had chosen to leave behind. I had cried my way to Kenya, agonising over whether I had made the right choice, leaving Sarah for this ride. I had missed her and longed to phone, yet knew that the sound of her voice would have pushed me straight to the nearest airport. I had woken in the pitch black, cool and silent desert nights, convinced that I had heard her voice or felt her beside me. But there was never anybody there. Not a day went by when I did not question what I was doing. In some ways my wonderful adventure had been the worst eight months of my life. It had certainly been the saddest and the loneliest. But we both knew that I had had to go away; I needed to do it. Now, in Kenya, I tried to turn my daydreams forwards to thoughts of the excitement and challenges of the Americas and Asia.

I rode, robbery free, into Nairobi where I met a concentration of fascinating characters unmatched anywhere else on my ride. I ended up staying three weeks. Ewart Grogan, the first person to traverse the length of Africa (to impress a girl, of course) wrote of 'the men who dared to stand clear and crisp above the trivial vapours of the age'. Nairobi was full of them, people 'who travelled a short while towards the sun, and left the vivid air signed with their honour'. I felt like a Spirograph as I went round and round and round, never quite knowing where I was headed or who I would meet next, or what they would dazzle me with: tales of lifetimes in wild places from artists, authors, soldiers, hunters, charmers and taunting beauties. Round and round in unpredictable twists and lunges and yet when you stop and look you see a beautiful shape that all makes sense. The group of friends, and the friends of those friends, and their friends, that I stumbled into in Nairobi was a tingling rush of mad people, who lived and laughed and loved with the fizzing energy of a Roman candle. I met no boring people, endured no dull dinners of painfully unimaginative questioning. Bacon sizzled and champagne popped high on the lip of the Great Rift Valley for a memorable breakfast with one family, again friends of friends, who were particularly kind to me in Nairobi. I met a man who had flown a tiny plane to New Zealand, someone organising a relay race around the world, a camel expert, an artist who climbed Kilimanjaro carrying a mop to paint her canvases with, a casino gambler, a woman who crossed Sudan on a camel, colonial lion-hunter types and a charming chap who almost punched my lights out for beating him at pool. These people did not exist; they lived.

A pair of amusing and mad middle-aged women decided they should find me a girl. After much entertaining and bitchy gossip about the relative charms, availabilities and dimensions of Nairobi's youth they settled on one name. I was whisked off on an immediate and painfully contrived shopping expedition to purchase, urgently, a milk jug from the unsuspecting victim's shop. And so followed the world's first ever attempt at matchmaking in the midst of a pottery shop. Memorable, hilarious, embarrassing and totally unsuccessful. The woman was beautiful, really beautiful. My bicycle, grubby T-shirt and flip-flops made it a non-starter. It was probably just as well: I found out later that her boyfriend (who owned a jet and a ranch) had a tendency to beat the crap out of anyone who so much as bought a milk jug from his girl. Somebody had gone recently to his father to complain about his endless boorish behaviour. Father promptly punched the visitor.

This comfortable lifestyle I was so relishing left me feeling pains of guilt and a kind of dishonesty whenever I passed in a car through Nairobi's slum areas. Drivers locked the doors and I looked out feeling a sense of betrayal. Most of my time in Africa was amongst people who lived lives far poorer, materially, than my own, yet I normally felt comfortable and at ease when I was on my bike. Now, in a nice air-conditioned car, I felt uncomfortable because, no matter how hard I tried to pretend otherwise, I was well aware of the privilege that I could always escape from my self-imposed life of poverty whenever it became too difficult.

Planning adventures is much more fun than actually undertaking them: lying on the floor poring over maps, dunking cookies in mugs of steaming tea, lost in happy, heroic daydreams. I was planning to cycle through the Democratic Republic of Congo. Generally speaking, countries with 'Democratic' in their title are not very. I had to find out the feasibility of such a route through regions ruined by war. Calling the Embassy was frustrating and chaotic, for I was repeatedly redirected by the switchboard to a local bookshop who seemed well accustomed to this. Eventually I got through to someone at the Embassy who said that I must come along in person for a visa interview. Everyone else in Kenya told me that I would be a fool to ride where war had already cost four million lives. I trekked down to the DRC Embassy for my interview and was told straight away that I would not be given a visa for the east of the country. Perhaps it was actually somebody in the bookshop who had told me to go to the Embassy in person just so that I would leave them alone. DRC was off the plan and the relief I felt told me that this decision was probably wise.

Beryl Markham, the first woman to fly across the Atlantic, described the Muthaiga Club in her book *West with the Night*: 'Its broad lounge, its bar, its dining room – none so elaborately furnished as to make a rough-handed hunter pause at its door, nor yet so dowdy as to make a diamond pendant swing ill at ease – were rooms in which the people who made the Africa I knew danced and talked and laughed, hour after hour.' I was in this ultimate symbol of Colonialism as a guest of the fun family I stayed with in Karen, the affluent suburb of Nairobi named for Karen Blixenith us was Kuki Gallmann, whose autobiography, *I Dreamed of Africa*, was filmed with Kim Basinger in the lead role. We argued amicably over the quotation she took her book title from. Later she invited me to visit her home, far from the nearest road.

The view from her friend's tiny plane was thrilling as we rose above Nairobi and flew out into the bush towards her house. Up, above the sprawling confusion of mud paths and rusting tin roofs of slums squashed intimately close against large homes with pretty lawns and tall security fences. Low, over the striped regularity of verdant coffee and tea plantations that nestled the hidden roofs of secret gems like the Heaths' home in Ruiru. The shadow of the plane leaped and jerked across the folds of the earth below us. Mount Kenya stood clear in the sunshine as I looked around the plane. There was not much to look at. It was tiny, old, and an alarmingly large proportion of the plane was made from wood or held with duct tape. The pilot, Eric, was aged about 60, dressed in khaki and armed with an iron handshake. The joystick rested nonchalantly between his knees. He dozed as we flew, waking when the plane wobbled and calmly re-adjusting the controls. As we passed above animals he became more animated, banking and circling low above a shuffling herd of elephants and pointing out the lolloping, rocking run of giraffe alarmed by the plane. Flying directly above a line of wildebeest it was easy to recognise them from their neat wildebeest-shaped shadows flat on the ground. Soon we were approaching Kuki's home, with no other building visible in any direction, and bumping down on the rough grassy landing strip and taxiing right to her front door where we were greeted by Kuki's six Alsatian dogs. Number 7, I was told, had sadly become leopard food just last week.

I spent a special few days on Kuki's 100,000 acre Ol Ari Nyiro ranch that is dedicated to cultural, educational and environmental research. I walked for hours with Eric to inspect beehives made from hollow logs jammed in high tree forks or to check the water level in dams, walking quietly and listening carefully. We stood still to let elephant and buffalo pass by and turned back from one path when a lion roared ahead. I accompanied the anti-poaching unit tracking the footprints of a man and an elephant up dramatic ridges, steep gorges and open savannah, across valleys and plains. The local tribe, the Pokot, prove their manliness in no uncertain way by spearing elephants by hand. Excellent for impressing girls, less so for impressing conservationists. When heavy rain wiped away the tracks we had been following we were forced to give up the chase. We hiked back to base and piled into an open-backed jeep to visit the local chief and discuss this latest clash of interests. We had to stop often to leap out and slash through bushes with machetes and push the vehicle through sucking mud. It was a couple of hours before we arrived in the village, a cluster of remote huts and people standing idle. After negotiations with the chief, which the frustrated wardens told me would achieve nothing (compared to the National Police policy of shooting poachers on sight), we raced back towards the ranch to try and beat the rainstorm that we could see brewing on the horizon.

I was surprised, on the plane back to Nairobi, at a sudden pulsing of vivid snapshots racing into my mind. They were not, as I might have expected, visions of wild Africa. Instead they were a fairly random collection of innocuous moments from my ride. A roundabout in Syria, swimming in the Danube, Istanbul's grand bazaar, a derelict factory in Romania, buying lentils in Slovakia, camping in a rainy forest, the neat number plates of Luxembourg, the motor bikers who wished me good luck as I disembarked in Calais, the Red Sea at sunset, cold fog and mud in Serbia (or was it Turkey), juggling firesticks in Jordan, the church in Eztergom, Hungary, camping in an almond grove in Bulgaria... I could not explain or predict the surfacing of random memories from among the millions that my ride was generating.

It really was time to ride again. Kenya was full of people who had come for a fortnight and stayed a lifetime. That was going to happen to me unless I escaped soon. I said my reluctant goodbyes and pedalled south. It was midday and the sun was on my back. This confused me as I was so used to riding towards the noon sun, until I remembered that I was in the southern hemisphere now where the noon sun is in the north. A man beside the road out of Nairobi was selling second-hand toilets. At least he had something to sit on whilst waiting for a customer. "Long safari?" he asked, simply, as I passed. "Long safari," I replied.

Africa as I Had Hoped

People are about as happy as they decide
that they are going to be.
Abraham Lincoln

Through southern Kenya and Tanzania I grew nervous about wild camping. Normally I simply pulled off the road where nobody could see me, but I had started to worry about wild animals. Hearing the sawing huff and puff of a leopard one dark night instantly persuaded me to get back in the habit of spending nights in villages.

The good-humoured Maasai never minded me pitching my tent in their villages once I had asked permission from the chief. They took pride in caring for me. I pitched my tent outside the huts on the immaculately swept earth then showed the inevitable curious crowd how I put up my tent, how I cooked and so on. The universal exclamation of surprise in Africa is a high pitched, drawn out *'eeeh!'* and most things I did triggered shrill choruses of *'eeeh!'* and laughter. The elasticated tent poles, the inflatable camping mattress, the penknife, the petrol stove… The routine of my life was new and entertaining for them. I would invite the small children to have a go in my tent but they were always too shy until one tiny brave soul would pick up the courage to try it for size. Chaos erupted as, of course, all of them then wanted a go.

I felt completely at ease in these most un-English of settings. The World Cup was only a week away and I was excited, but nobody there knew anything about it. We had so little in common. The language barrier was frustrating but entertaining as I tried to decipher and answer questions through charades and drawings. My inflatable globe helped explain my route and a letter that I had had translated into Swahili explained the reasons for my ride. My maps excited and confused everyone and it was fun to watch men arguing about where they were on the map. Most had never used a map and had no idea how to read them. At times in Africa I made the mistake of thinking that because I could not communicate with someone that they were stupid. Of course the stupidity was mine for not speaking their language, but I never felt this in the cheerful homesteads of the Maasai where communication always seemed possible.

Maasai men are incredibly vain. Primping, preening and strutting with all the confidence of the King's Road, they were fascinated by my blond straight hair, whilst I was equally intrigued by the size of the holes in their earlobes. I hope that if I return one day to Tanzania, I will find villages where the fashion for men's hair is straight blond, rather than dyed red. I enjoyed my evenings with the Maasai. They had too much dignity and self-sufficiency to care, or at least to ask, about my wealth and were happy simply for me to be spending an evening with them.

As night fell the boys returned to the villages from the savannah with the cattle herds. The sun set, quickly and fiercely, and thorn bushes were pulled into a barricade around the villages to protect the people and the cattle in their wooden pens from wild animals. Children bounced and scampered all around, occasionally cuffed with good humour if they were too noisy. Babies cried with terror when they saw me and their mothers laughed as they comforted them. Women crouched over smoky cooking fires, using cow dung for fuel, and men sat outside their huts and chatted. The huts were made of mud, sticks, grass and cow dung and urine. Some of the men had dyed red hair and big holes in their ears. Women, with shaved heads,wore earrings dangling like chandeliers with mini-spears hanging at the bottom of them.

An absolutely beautiful woman, Esupat, took me round her village one evening. She showed me the snorting cattle, the piles of skinny firewood, her friends and her family, and all the small details of her life. She was taller than me and as she smiled down, wild Flashman thoughts burst through my brain. I could jack in my ride, marry Esupat, and become a warrior. Instead we returned to my bike and I set up my tent which everyone, as always, found very funny. If the Maasai had a *Discovery Channel*, I would be on it. Esupat's little sister brought me a low stool and a cup of milky tea and then fled, giggling. The evenings ended early; there were no lights or even lanterns in the villages so I would be in my tent early, falling asleep to the dull clunking of wooden cowbells.

There is a jubilation at feeling like the only person in the world, cycling carefree down a cool road at dawn. It was good to be free. I felt lucky to have the time to lie back on the earth watching clouds metamorphose in the sky, to watch ants enjoying my breadcrumbs, to listen to the wind in the yellow grass and feel it fresh on my sweat. I saw a snake get run over by a car. Its mouth was wide but silent as its body writhed and flipped, red blood splashing onto the tarmac. Plains stretched ahead towards Mount Meru, seductively and tantalisingly glimpsed through the clouds. Kilimanjaro was stubbornly buried beneath the duvet of the rainy season. I knew it was there, I knew what it looked like but I gazed hopefully at nothing but clouds. Instead I saw some Marabou storks, possibly the ugliest bird on earth. Their heads are pink and stubbly, like a sunburned and almost bald old man. Their beaks are drab and enormous. They stand an imposing 150 centimetres tall with a vast wingspan. A pink sac hangs from their throat. I imagined a conversation amongst birds: 'Excuse me, mister, you appear to have something dangly and grotesque stuck on your chin…' 'Oh, it's part of your face, is it? I am sorry.'

The road towards Arusha climbed gradually, too gently to see the gradient but enough to feel it. I kept stopping to check my brakes, sure that something was rubbing and slowing me down. A signpost told me that Arusha was exactly halfway between Cairo and Cape Town. I stayed there with Jo, a primary school teacher from England, and spoke at her school. Jo had a giant bird outfit at home, which she needed to return to the school. She decided to wear the costume and cycle into school. I followed behind, fascinated to see the reaction of locals to a huge bird cycling through their town: nobody batted an eyelid. It confirmed my theory that they thought that foreigners were so completely weird that nothing would surprise them.

Jo's husband, Ben, was a bush safari pilot. He told me of a fellow pilot who had wanted to leave his job, but his boss would not allow it. When he was due to fly a safari group, he sat anonymously in the back of the plane with the other passengers. Grumbling got under way about the pilot being late, and the pilot said, 'Geez, it can't be that hard!' He jumped into the cockpit, fiddled theatrically with the controls and took off. The screaming, terrified passengers did not appreciate the joke and, as he had hoped, the pilot found himself unemployed.

Dirty children stared at me or, unaware of my passing, continued playing football with bound balls of rags. Men sat around in contorted postures of idleness. I saw, more than once, a man asleep in a wheelbarrow, a brilliantly symbolic gesture. I camped one night, with the permission of Mr. Ngoma, the teacher, outside a school. I was woken early surrounded by a giggling mass of young children who squealed and whooped as I danced for them before packing up my tent and waving goodbye. On the road ladies, graceful and poised, carried huge bunches of bananas balanced on their heads and babies strapped to their backs. Their arms swung slowly and their big bums wiggled in colourful dresses, called *khangas*. One woman, empty-handed, walked with her handbag perched on her head. A teenaged girl carried an enormous bundle of sugarcane on her head and I stopped to ask her if I could have a try. I could barely lift the pile on to my head and, once there, it felt like it was crushing my skull. I stumbled a couple of paces before giving up. Children walked to school with books in plastic bags and their water for the day in old oil bottles swinging on string.

I always liked to camp under the full moon and try to remember where I had been for each full moon of my ride. A couple of days ride from the coast I sat at dusk in a small hollow, studying my World Cup schedule until the herder boys homeward plodded their weary way, shooing and shouting at their bony cattle, throwing pebbles at the stragglers. They left the world to darkness and to me and I wheeled my bike away from the road and rolled out my sleeping bag as my tenth full moon rose and silhouetted Meru and Kilimanjaro.

The elaborately painted buses in Tanzania with slogans such as 'Yo Boyz, 'God be with us,' and 'Born to die,' did nothing to change my perception that they were little more than lethal death traps driven by nutters. Within one hour I saw buses decorated with portraits of Bill Clinton, Saddam Hussein and Kofi Annan. I felt sure there was some sort of coded message in this high speed, smoky triumvirate. (Elsewhere I saw the Queen and also a smiling Alex Ferguson carrying the red briefcase of the Chancellor of the Exchequer.)

Lunatic mini-bus taxis, *dala dalas*, raced the streets, swerving round roundabouts (known amusingly as *keep-a-leftys*) crammed full with passengers. There was always room for one more, and the drivers swerved to a halt whenever someone flagged them down. This was normally about once every 10 seconds. While the new passenger squeezed himself inside, the driver floored the accelerator, pushing back into the traffic and overtaking everything possible before slamming on his brakes again to pick up yet another person a hundred yards down the road. You could get on or off whenever you wanted to, so long as the driver heard you above his thumping music. The driver always had a buddy who collected fares and shouted and whistled for business from his macho position standing in the open doorway and leaning out over the road. I had numerous, near-death close shaves with *dala dalas*.

The road was also busy with cyclists and as our paths crossed I was kept busy dinging my greetings on my bell and giving the cheery thumbs-up greeting that seems to die out in England once you grow too old to give thumbs-up signs to lorry drivers out of the back window of the school bus and progress to showing your bottom instead. Men wrapped in red robes clutching spears whizzed past. My bell was put to shame by the Tanzanians', who often modified them so that, when pressed, a lever would rub on the rim of the wheel making a continuous ringing sound. Flasher characters fitted battery-powered horns to their bikes and I followed behind one chap who, oblivious of my presence, kept playing over and over his horn that played the Happy Birthday tune. The bikes were laden with firewood, bananas or drums of water. Many also carried a passenger. The bicycle is the most efficient mode of transport ever invented, environmentally friendly and cheap. A bicycle does the equivalent of 3,000 miles per gallon, is more efficient than a gazelle or an eagle and can carry 10 times its own weight, something that no aeroplane can manage. They are simple and cheap and really improve the standard of living in rural Africa.

The World Cup, at last, was only hours away. France, the World Champions, were playing Senegal, the African lions, in the opening match of the competition. I said goodbye to the latest village that had looked after me, memorable for the children's homemade wooden bicycles, and pedalled quickly to find a town with a television where I could watch the football. Each village I reached told me that the next village would have a television. But none of them did. After four years waiting I was going to miss the match. I was desperate and so, with only two hours to go until kick-off, I cheated.

You may want to stop reading now and demand a refund for this book that claims that I cycled to South Africa. Because I did not. I cheated. I stuck out my thumb, a pick-up stopped, I thanked the driver, hurled my bike in the back, and whizzed – entirely voluntarily – 60 miles to Dar Es Salaam. I had no excuse and no regrets. A game of football was more important to me than sixty miles of flat scrubland. I never did it again, but once is enough.

Five minutes before kick off I was cycling, panic rising once more, up and down the streets of Dar Es Salaam trying to find a television. "Television? Football?" I kept asking. Fortunately everyone understood those two words and pointed me in the right direction. I spotted a little board with 'France-Senegal' scrawled on it. Relieved, I pushed my bike through into a scruffy little backroom bar and flopped, sweat-soaked, onto a chair. Welcome to The Greatest Show on Earth.

Twelve people were sitting in silence round a small television screen on pink plastic chairs in the courtyard at the back of the *shebeen*, or drinking den. I bought a Pepsi and sat down. The screen was half obscured by bright sunlight. One supporter spoke English and checked that I was going to be supporting Senegal. Of course, I told him. The referee blew his whistle and the game began, a momentous game in which the African nation, in their first ever World Cup, defeated the reigning World champions.

Early in the second half of the match the phone rang behind the bar. The call was for me. Surprised, I walked to the bar. Who could possibly want to speak to me in a random African boozer? Nobody I had ever known knew where I was.

"Hello?" I asked.

"My friend," spoke an African man with a deep, rolling voice. "After the game you will be beaten and robbed. Stay behind for 10 minutes before you leave in order to be safe."

Before I could speak again he hung up.

I returned to my seat beside my bike and looked around. Everyone was watching the game. Nobody was doing anything unusual or looking at me. What the hell was going on?

I didn't want to leap up and panic. But I didn't want to hang around either. Who on earth was that on the phone? (I found a moment to be amused that I was not going to be robbed until the game was actually over: 'Police are today looking for a dangerous gang of robbers. They are all believed to be keen football fans…'). I started to wonder whether the caller was actually trying to make me stay behind so that I could be mugged then. I had to get out of there, to the safety of the public street. I looked around the courtyard, searching for escape routes if things suddenly kicked off. I could probably leap onto that table and then up onto the roof, but where then? I would just have to take my chances.

I drank my Pepsi, watched the game and tried not to let on that I had been tipped off. I was scared stiff. With 10 minutes of the game remaining I stood up as calmly as I could and wheeled my bike towards the exit. My whole body was tensed and expecting the scrape of chairs as I was rushed and grabbed and punched. Here we go. Oh no. Oh no, no, no, no, *NO!* I was ready to kick and bite and scratch or to run – hopefully to run. But nobody moved from the television and, after sauntering out the door, I jumped onto my bike and pedalled like I had never pedalled before. I didn't care where I was going, I was just going. I stood on the pedals and thrashed them round and round as I raced down the road, snatching glances back over my shoulder. After a few minutes the lactic acid started to bite and I slowed down, certain by now that nobody was following me and I was safe again. It was a strange and inexplicable incident.

With shaking legs I rode slowly through the city to find the International School where I had been invited to stay in return for talking to the children. I stayed with Shannon, a music teacher from Vancouver, and tried vainly to enthuse her about the soccer. Staying with complete strangers for a week or more, I always worried that as soon as I left they would dance a jig of delight that I was gone. So I was happy that Shannon invited me to stay with her if I rode through Canada.

The next morning saw me, just before kick off for the Ireland-Cameroon match, cycling round the mansions of the embassy district by the softly lapping Indian Ocean and the palm trees and searching, once again, for a television. Paradise is no place to watch football. I found a bar just in time in a backstreet district. It was 9.30am and the beer was flowing. Men were tearing at hunks of chewy goat gristle, the ever popular *nyama choma,* and cheering the game. Across the bottom of the screen scrolled a message: 'If you are watching this outside Mozambique it is an illegal broadcast.' Nobody cared. Street kids who earned pennies cleaning shoes stood in the doorway with their brushes and watched the match. A man translated the newspaper headlines of yesterday's match for me: 'Goooooal! Senegal brave, France like a tomato.' When Cameroon scored the street children danced and cheered. There is solidarity for all African teams not found in Europe. The setting for watching England's matches was rather different. I went with some ex-pats to the smart Sheraton Hotel which, extraordinarily and foolishly, was offering free beer to English football supporters courtesy of British Airways. I planned to leave Dar and get back on the bike the morning after the England-Argentina match. But the free beer and David Beckham's penalty winner combined to hit me with a monster hangover. I went to the beach with Shannon instead and resolved to leave the next morning.

Tanzania exactly matched my dreams of riding in Africa. Friendly people, scary animals, magnificent landscapes, ferocious sunsets and a jovial, shambolic atmosphere. The road wound past forested hills, meadows of white flowers, clusters of aloes, outcrops of rock and many baobab trees. The iconic baobab tree, with its vast, stubby water-storing trunks and mesh of thin, root-like branches is known as the 'upside-down tree'. A Bushman myth explains how God, at the beginning of time, gave a tree to each animal to plant. The hyena, last in line, was so annoyed at the weird-looking baobab he received that he planted it upside-down in disgust.

In the Mikumi National Park a sign warned: 'DANGER. Wild Animals next 50 kilometres.' This was the only road towards Malawi so I had to continue. It was perhaps the only 50 kilometres of Africa where I was not sharing the road with other cyclists and pedestrians. That morning a Maasai man had done superb impressions for me of all the animals that I may encounter in Mikumi. Foolishly I reassured myself that if

I pedalled fast I would be OK. A lorry stopped and the driver wound down his window,

"Hey, *mzungu,* are you a crazy man?! Come in my lorry. This place is no good for a bicycle!"

"I know," I smiled, "but I am riding very fast."

"*Mzungu,*" he shook his head, "the *simba* (lion) is very, very fast!"

And he drove on.

Fifty kilometres later I was out of puff. Fortunately I had not seen any lions, and I had enjoyed the not-so-scary giraffes, zebras, warthogs, baboons and impala. I rested in a café, enjoying a cup of tea and a chapatti in the company of Christopher, a 54-year-old English-speaking Maasai. He was decked out in full Maasai regalia and his knobkerry club rested against my knee. His cup of tea was too hot to drink and so he poured some into his saucer to cool and then slurped it from there, exactly as my Latin teacher used to do at school. From the seat of a bicycle the world felt painfully large and yet the more of it I saw the more I was amazed at its smallness and similarities.

The road wound up precariously towards a forested horizon. I swept down hills clutching my sunhat, and struggled up the hills cursing my fast disintegrating gears that jumped and slipped. Several lorries now knew me along this road as they passed back and forth from Dar Es Salaam to the interior. They beeped and waved whenever they passed, picking up my resolve a little each time.

For a week or so every village I passed through had a new, pristine mosque, which was by far the smartest building in the village. One man told me they nicknamed them 'Osama Mosques' as they had been funded by Saudi Arabia. I was disappointed when the man said that he would have liked to invite me to his home but that I would be unable to eat African food as it was not good enough for white people. I rode on and camped alone, and ate old bread and jam in my tent.

Dawn was cold and dewy, to my surprise, and I realised that

I must have climbed quite high as I put my socks on my hands to act as gloves. I preferred cold toes to cold fingers. I was having bike problems again. Four spokes had broken so my back wheel was very buckled but the tool I needed to replace them had also broken. Ahead of me stood a wall of purple mountains, and as I climbed towards them the wheel finally buckled and would no longer rotate. For a couple of hours I tried to improvise repairs before summoning the motivation to hitchhike back into Mbeya to search for a solution.

Walking round from one red herring to another, I was eventually directed towards a garage on the edge of town. My hopes were not high, so I was surprised and excited when a mechanic watched my charade explaining the problem, walked to the back of the garage and returned with a wheel that would fit on my bike. It even had five gears: good news as I thought of the ridge of peaks that still awaited. Perhaps relief was etched too obviously on my face because the garage fixed a high price for the wheel and, even after haggling, I still had to pay £20, a whole month's budget for living. The wheel was poor quality so I decided I would strap my original to the back of the bike and hope that I could get a replacement spoke tool from England.

David, a guy I met in Dar, had invited me to stay on a tea plantation that night, but wasting most of the day fixing my wheel had left me with a long way still to ride, and I was in a grump at the broken tool and at paying so much for a rubbish wheel. So, as soon as I got back on the road, I set myself to the hard 2,500 metres climb for the pass as the sun set. My back brake did not fit on the new wheel, so I slowed myself with my feet on the downhills. The air was deliciously cool, rice fields changed colour with the breeze like rubbing velvet, trees and crops reminded me of home: peas, potatoes, cabbage. I pedalled on into the darkness that falls so suddenly near the equator, my senses tingling with awareness of the hazards in the darkness, of potholes on the steep descents, of badly-lit vehicles and of the ease with which I could be followed and robbed. I pedalled fast through villages and lines of roadside food stalls. I smelt barbecuing corn cobs and sour maize beer. Naked light bulbs and cooking fires gave glimpses of evening routine. At about 9 o'clock I saw the sign for the Wakulima Tea Company and turned down a dirt track to find David.

Next thing I remember, I was waking up under a fat duvet, in a bed, by a window that looked out over acres and acres of squat tea bushes. The fragile morning mist hazed the blue hills that rolled down to Lake Malawi. My breath condensed in the highland air and I decided that a couple more hours sleep would be an excellent idea.

When I eventually got out of bed David had long since left for work on the tea estate. I was happy to sit at the kitchen table, catch up my diary, watch the World Cup and read my book. There was an old record player in the living room and I felt that here I had a good excuse to play some Dire Straits, if indeed an excuse is ever needed: 'These mist covered mountains, are a home now for me.'

A muddy haul through the tea plantations and a thrilling twenty mile swooping downhill took me into Malawi – country number 20 – and the first free border crossing since Europe. Malawi is a small, slender country flanked by Lake Malawi. Following independence in the 1960's, Dr. Kamuzu Banda became President for Life of the country. Malawi's first multi-party elections were then not held until 1994. Corruption, over-population, poverty and AIDS are severely testing the resolve of a people with a reputation as the friendliest in Africa. Life expectancy in Malawi was falling steadily: it was now less than forty years.

Haggling with a black market moneychanger at the border, I thought I had achieved the impossible and actually succeeded in ripping *him* off. As I argued with him and the price fell I felt like I had out-Heroded Herod and I rode into Malawi very pleased with myself. It was a couple of hours later that it dawned on me that I had in fact got my ratios the wrong way round and had actually haggled myself out of a few extra dollars. The moneychanger must have been too confused by my stupidity to have seized the initiative and press his advantage.

In Malawi I hit the well-worn backpacker trail. Hostels boasted pizzas, milkshakes and banana pancakes and weary *mzungu* faces whizzed past daily on buses. I celebrated the expansion in culinary options in my traditional manner, with more jam sandwiches, sticks of sugarcane and occasional treats of *ugali*, called *nsima* in Malawi, or rice and beans from roadside stalls.

I pushed ahead to the large town of Mzuzu, where I could be sure of finding a television for the England-Brazil match. For three days I rode fast all day, and for a couple of hours into the night. I slept beside my bike in roadside bushes, rose at 4am and was off again, riding into the dawn, thinking of how few sunrises I was ever conscious to relish back home. If England failed to beat Brazil, it certainly was not going to be because of *my* lack of commitment! I made it to Mzuzu in driving rain with 10 minutes to spare. The match was a disaster, England surrendered feebly and our World Cup was over. I had four more years to wait for the next attempt, and I hoped that I would be home by then.

I was on my way to talk at Kamuzu Academy. The school, known as the 'Eton of Africa', was incongruous enough in itself but, surrounded by villages of destitute people, it was absolutely extraordinary. The school was founded by former President Kamuzu Banda in the style of an English public school. Pupils, the children of wealthy government officials or bright children on scholarships, studied the British Curriculum, including Latin and Greek, and wore uniforms and straw boaters as they walked the cloistered courtyards. Built in the village of the dictator's birth, with its chapel, ornamental lake, Olympic-sized swimming pool and golf course, the school consumed almost the whole Malawi education budget. After Banda's death the school was forced to adapt and become a private, fee-paying enterprise. I was curious to discover whether Kamuzu Academy would seem like a beacon of what could be achieved in an increasingly desperate continent, or just another demonstration of African leaders' corruption and money-wasting. I was so tired of examples of the latter that I was glad to manhandle and squeeze the Eton of Africa into the former category in my mind.

I rode beside a wide, inviting river that had almost run its course. Downstream I could see Lake Malawi, deep blue and demanding to be swum in. Out of the far shore rose steep, rough mountains, bluer than the sky but lighter than the lake. A stripe of thin white cloud hung halfway up them. I camped in a field of sugarcane by the lake. As the sun set, I relaxed with a delicious blend of Malawi gold.

Neat, thatched cottages stood in swept clearings alongside small plots of vegetables. The bark of rubber trees was scored in spirals and streams of the white rubber sap oozed down the trees and was collected in cut-off Coke bottles. I steadily ate peanuts as I rode, spitting out the shells. Patient ladies sat beside the road selling little piles of tiny fish from the critically over-fished lake. At dusk heavy dugout canoes would take to the water, using large paraffin lamps to lure fish to the surface. The canoes worked in groups of three, one carrying the lamp and two other canoes circling with their net. They worked until moonrise when they returned to shore with their catch. The fishermen spent their days carving canoes with axes, drying fish on long tables and mending their nets. Lots of them called out "Give me money" but with smiling faces that expressed hope rather than expectance. After Ethiopia they did not faze me in the slightest!

People driving back to Lilongwe from Lake Malawi kept their purchases and their car fresh by hanging their fish on string from the wing mirrors. Roadside treats included boiled mice on sticks and plucked baby birds. I disappointed myself by being too squeamish to take advantage of these extremely cheap dinner-party-conversation-enhancing foodstuffs. Montaigne said: 'Every man calls barbarous that to which he is not accustomed.'

Suddenly men were standing across the road, demanding that I stop. Barefoot and wearing rags they wore bags on their heads like balaclavas and brandished bows and arrows. Trouble.

I smiled, waved hello, and pedalled like hell as I closed the gap between them and me. No way would I stop. I burst through their line and they started to chase. I smiled and waved even more and pedalled in terror until they gave up. About an hour later the same thing happened again and as I put on a sprint and scattered the men aside, I saw people in a nearby roadside café laughing at my fright. I braked and pulled up to the café. They explained that the gangs were only out to collect cash for parties on Malawi Day, their Independence Day, on July 6th, and that it was all just good-natured fun. A man handed me a Pepsi to apologise for their laughter and I soon saw the funny side of it all. I suppose that I felt as a Malawian would were he to be accosted in England, early November, by a bunch of boys with something resembling a corpse in a wheelbarrow, demanding cash before hurling the effigy onto a roaring fire.

REPUBLICA DE MOÇAMBIQUE

Visto Nº 57691|LL|2002

Passaporte Nº S00320963

Categoria:

Tipo SIMPLES

Utilizável de 13 07 2002

13 09 2002

Autorizado a permanecer

30, TRINTA DIAS

dias apartir da data de entrada.

LILONGUE 10.07.2002

Assinatura

VASMOSEL
DIRECTO A ...

No Time for Romance

There's lots of pretty girls in Mozambique,
And plenty time for good romance.
Bob Dylan

Arno had ridden into Jordan with Simon and me, and he now flew to Lilongwe to ride with me for his summer holiday. He brought the freewheel tool I needed to repair my wheel, as well as chocolate and other welcome goodies. In a hardware store in Lilongwe the Indian owner kindly gave me a new front derailleur that I needed. But after hours of faffing it still did not work. Free it may have been, but crap it certainly was. It looked as though I would have to continue changing gear with an old toothbrush until I reached South Africa, reaching down as I pedalled and using the toothbrush to push the chain from gear to gear. This amused Arno. I told him that schadenfreude was a German word, and that it was therefore unbecoming for a Frenchman. That we English certainly did not feel the need for such a word. He was still amused. "Bloody Frenchman," I cursed loudly as he sped past me. He turned around, grinned and gave me his best Gallic shrug. His plan was to ride with me to Botswana. It was good to see him again.

The road towards Mozambique shrank to no more than a sandy footpath through the bush. The border at Vila Nova de Frontera was just a shell of ruined buildings, a run-down reminder of the days of Portuguese control, days of electricity, running water, paved roads and a workable infrastructure. It was the first and only border crossing in the world where anyone tried to make me pay a bribe. The scruffy, unpleasant-looking officer invented a fee that Arno and I must pay. Smiling politely, we refused. Scowling, he ordered us to pay. Smiling politely, we refused. A game that could have continued for quite some time. I had considerably more time than money and I would have smiled angelically at him all day. Eventually he realised that he had picked the wrong opponents. He angrily stamped our passports and gestured us to leave. He seemed amazed to have found two foreigners who were not flush with easy cash. Outside the police gates a loitering money changer tried to rip us off by a factor of 100. Did we really look that stupid? I spoke Spanish in a Russian accent, in an attempt to speak Portuguese. Perhaps, listening to my 'Portuguese', he figured that we did.

Mozambique had been a Portuguese colony until 1975, when it became independent after a 10 year conflict. The last decades have been tough. When the Portuguese fled, the country was left in a terrible state. An example of the chaos is that of Mozambique's 500 doctors, only 80 remained after independence. The new left-wing, single-party government were also fighting a rebel group, backed by South Africa and Rhodesia. Up to a million people were killed in the latest civil war, many millions more were displaced, and the already fragile infrastructure of the country was totally destroyed.

After the war years, drought led to famine for millions. The country, staggering and collapsing, saw peace at last only in 1992. Vast floods at the turn of the millennium further damaged Mozambique's attempts to stand back on her own feet. People do not expect to outlive their forties and, for most, the future is bleak. The gold beaches, warm sapphire shallows and pearl-like islands of the tourist-loved coast seem incongruous against the brutally tough interior. A beautiful necklace sparkling on the throat of a dying woman. It was yet another nation that had only really drifted across the periphery of my consciousness, a whiff of pity and guilt from the TV news before I returned to my supper with the heavy feeling that 'there is nothing to do about anything, and now it is nearly time for the news. We must listen to the weather report, and the international catastrophes.'

Choosing campsites in Mozambique was difficult. There is an ever-present threat from a million landmines. Mosquitoes whined and dined and sweat stung our eyes as we searched for somewhere to sleep in the dusk. Nights in Mozambique were all stewing humidity and torturing choruses of mosquitoes as grating as primary school recorder recitals. We decided that fire probably blows up landmines and so camped on the blackened remains of bush fires. I later asked a friend who works for the HALO Trust, a landmine charity, what he thought of our theory. He laughed.

Riding ahead, Arno was a dusty silhouette in the sunset as we arrived in Caia, an unusual-looking town for Africa, showing its Portuguese influences with a plaza and walled mercado. We stocked up on bread and oranges. The town wore the heavy label of 'faded glory', which was the overriding impression of most of Mozambique. Uncleared landmines had made parts of the town potentially lethal; trees grew from the shells of houses. Two hundred metres from the sunny spot where we sat eating oranges a child had been blown up recently.

Further into Mozambique we rode a remote road through scrubby bush with no traffic, no villages and worryingly little water. It was hot. Too hot. The sunny sky was aqua blue. We were pushing deeper into the bush, a giant, inhospitable expanse of nothingness. To an Englishman, relatively unaccustomed to the enormous wilds of Africa, it was a grim, unwelcoming, ugly land. And yet, for the few people who lived there, it was home, it was familiar normality. Occasionally we passed three or four huts on stilts with a few pigs and chickens shuffling around. It was one of the most grinding livelihoods I had seen. It was just survival. We stopped occasionally to ask for water but only accepted a single litre at a time: we did not know how far people had to walk or how deep they had to dig to find water.

Our communication attempts failed apart from understanding their shy smiles of welcome. We crouched down beside the naked people sitting outside their hut and politely proffered our water bottle. Three young boys ran off to fill it, fighting each other to carry it.

We were beginning to suspect that Bob Dylan had had more fun in Mozambique than us as we trudged through the days and miles. We discussed the perfect pizza to pass the time. Arno suggested toppings and I awarded a ring of my bell and a point for every suggestion I approved of.

"Olives!"

"Black or green?"

"Both?" Ding!

"Mushrooms and sweet peppers!" Ding!

"How do you say…. Les artichauts? And Parma ham!"

"Monsieur, you are a genius!" Ding! Ding!

"'Ow about ze salmon and feta cheese?" Ding! Ding!

The miles rolled by…

Later we competed to see who could cycle for the longest with their eyes closed.

We were going at impressive speed through the approaching darkness towards Chimoio. I was relishing my superb level of fitness to be able to ride as fast as this on a heavy bike after such a long day's ride. It was hard for me to remember what it was like being a person with merely ordinary fitness standards. Or so I smugly thought until a heavily-set, middle-aged gentleman in spectacles and a suit, carrying a briefcase and riding home from work on an old single-speed bike, pulled alongside us. "Is that a motorised machine, sir?" he asked before grilling us about life on the road.

The lights of Chimoio signalled the return to modern civilization. We were there because that morning a man in a passing car had stopped, given us his phone number, and offered us beds for the night. Unfortunately the number turned out to be incorrect so we were stuck in town, after dark, with nowhere to sleep. We could not find a campsite and ended up in the cheapest hotel in town. We wanted to share a single room to save money, but this brought an argument with the owner. He thought that we were gay, and did not want to let us stay at all. Word obviously got around because when I went to the toilet in the night I found the way back to the room blocked by a leering guy in tiny blue underpants, massaging his crotch and licking his lips at me. I slammed him against the wall, darted into the room and bolted the door behind me, not knowing whether to be revolted or amused.

It turned out to be good fortune that we hadn't camped, as a powerful storm lashed the night. We emerged into a morning of grey mist, cold fingers, tall sweet pine trees and fresh wet grass. After thousands of miles of dry African heat it was a beautiful change.

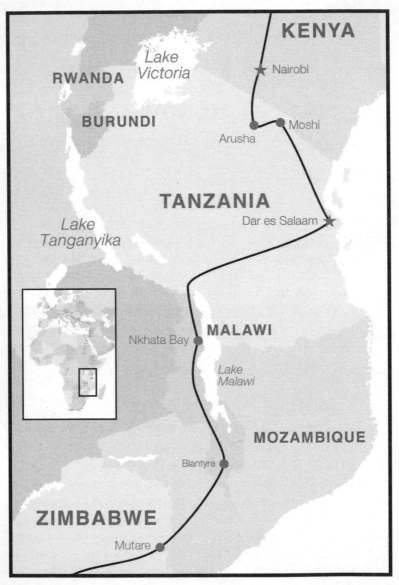

Large Problems in Zimbabwe

Africa's large problems are largely large Africans.
PJ O'Rourke

Vervet monkeys at the border post tried to steal a stick of sugarcane from my bike. I chased them off with my catapult, our new toys purchased in Malawi. Arno was an excellent shot with his but I only ever managed to hit a cow's backside and, twice, my own hand. I still have the scar. In no-man's land between Mozambique and Zimbabwe I managed to get the rear derailleur jammed in the wheel, even bending the bike frame in the process. Whilst Arno rode ahead into Mutare I had to walk, pushing Rita for 10 kilometres, striding through the golden late afternoon sun, winding up the mountain pass through verdant forest, listening to Verdi at full volume on the music player a friend had sent me. Over that pass lay Zimbabwe: the beginning of the end of the beginning. For so long I had been looking forward to arriving in Zim and I was not to be disappointed by the first impressions of ease and convenience. Mutare had paved roads and street signs, shops and restaurants, and everyone spoke English. My bike was mended efficiently, there was a cricket pitch, and they even had ice cream! I was so excited. After the rest of Africa, unable to drag itself out of poverty, Zimbabwe's infrastructure was a shining example.

Leaving Mutare there was a long, steep climb but I managed to grab the back of a passing lorry for a nice tow. Arno grabbed on too as the lorry overtook him and we bartered with the passenger in the back of the lorry over a price for being hauled up the pass. His insistence on an absurd fee backfired on him as in the end we simply let go at the top of the pass, and waved goodbye to him as the oblivious driver chugged on towards Harare.

The land was covered in *koppies*, huge round boulders jumbled on top of each other into improbable, conical, eye-catching hills. As the first stars pierced the evening light we climbed one of the *koppies*, the warmth of the day still radiating from the rocks like the memory of a dream. The rocks were decorated with ancient San Bushman rock paintings. Simple shapes of animals, the same animals of Africa that delight tourists today but that meant so much more to the person who created those paintings, who depended on those animals for life and for spiritual succour. I tried to imagine the delicate, light-skinned man who had sat on this same rock so long ago. His life had been a simple circle of seasons and a steady procession of years from childhood to adolescence to fatherhood and old age, unfettered by bills, borders or bureaucracy. A hard but simple life, I thought, a little enviously. Yet his life contained more than hunting, surviving and reproducing. For his art expressed an appreciation of beauty and a quest for meaning and fulfilment, an acknowledgement that there was more to life than mundane existing. And that aspect of his life is what has powerfully lived on, connecting with me through so many forgotten generations to my gently tracing, wondering fingers.

We passed neat farms on a smooth paved road with white lines and kilometre markers. Blue skies, a fresh breeze and shaded picnic spots. People waved at us from their cars. On the outside Zimbabwe still looked shiny and healthy. But the veneer of successful tranquility was no longer very deep in Zimbabwe. The farcical, guilt-inducing black market rate of exchange meant that everything was absurdly cheap for us as we changed our money on the streets at 10 times the official bank rate. This was the first sign to us that things were not as rosy as they used to be. The terrible slide into anarchy, racism, corruption, starvation and collapse was well on the way. We were in a country imploding in the hands of just one man.

It was not always this way. A fertile land for agriculture and mining, Zimbabwe was, until recent years, one of the most prosperous countries in Africa. Following a long civil war, the first free elections were held in 1980. Robert Mugabe won the election by a landslide, and optimism abounded for the future of Zimbabwe.

The one per cent of the population that was white no longer held power, but they did still hold the purse strings, owning 70 per cent of the country's arable land. But since 1999 land redistribution has been at the top of the political agenda as Mugabe began to rave and rage, blaming Colonial days for all his woes as age turned his mind and he showed no inclination to hand over power. Government racism flipped 180° after two peaceful decades; white farmers were forcibly removed from their land, and productivity crashed. Debt spiralled uncontrollably and famine scoured a country that was once an exporter of food. Zimbabwe was thrown out of the Commonwealth of Nations for election rigging and human rights abuses as the government eliminated opponents and silenced dissidents.

I was pessimistic about the future of Zimbabwe. The farmers I met agreed that land distribution amongst the people was indeed necessary, but that being thrown illegally from your family home to make way for one of the president's cronies was not the way to do it. Mugabe's campaign caused famine because food was no longer produced locally. People in Matabeleland were so desperate that they were beginning to cook and eat cow dung. I wonder how they felt about 'land liberation'? I was, yet again in Africa, riding through a land whose people were dying every day because of their corrupt rulers. Mugabe's wife allegedly holds the record for the most money spent on a single shopping visit to Harrod's. Robert Mugabe is killing Zimbabwe.

Over the past few months, people had been emailing me that Zimbabwe was currently too dangerous to ride through.

"Don't push your luck, Al."

"Things have changed since you were last there."

"You've been before, don't risk it now. Go through Zambia."

"Go through Mozambique instead."

"The country is nuts. Being white is the only excuse they need to do you over."

I never felt threatened in Zimbabwe. The people that I encountered were like most people in Africa: hard done by but stoical, hard up yet generous. Ordinary people who wanted only the freedom to get on with their lives. They wanted jobs not land. You do not learn much about the people of a country by looking at its leaders.

The focal issue for all Zimbabwe's woes was the ejection of white farmers from their land and on Heroes Day (August 12th), a day celebrating victory over the old white regime, President Robert Mugabe had this to say as he insisted that all whites must leave their land by the end of the month:

'Zimbabwe is for Zimbabweans... we are not for the British bidder... This is the land which, until now, was being held by sons of our colonial oppressors at our expense. This is the land which our victorious heroes could never desire to see remaining in the hands of the people they defeated... Colonialism came from the European Union... the wielders of those arms were Europeans, we now call farmers... Today, as we take our land, in the process settling the grievance of all grievances... we ask the so-called Free World these questions: do democracies enslave; do democracies colonise; do democracies discriminate, massacre, plunder and expropriate?... Britain, Europe and America can impose sanctions, or do worse devilish things... But we shall not budge; we shall not be deterred on this one question. The land is ours! Shame to them!... We know that our quarrel is with the former colonial power Britain and the British Government... We set for ourselves the deadline of end of August by which distribution of land ... resettlement should have been completed.'

One evening we approached a farm to ask if we could camp somewhere safe on their land. The owner was not home so the gardener phoned him. He said, with the spontaneous hospitality so typical of Africa, that we could certainly camp and that he would be home in a few hours. We relaxed on the lawn playing with his Rhodesian Ridgeback dogs. When Janie returned he invited us into his home and, over dinner, he spoke about the situation. Over years of hard work he had built his business up and bought, openly and legally, three farms. He had now been evicted from two of them without compensation, and was due to be kicked out of his remaining one. He spoke about the game parks, one of Zimbabwe's treasures, where the army were now wiping out whole herds of buffalo with machine guns to make a few quick bucks from selling the meat. He told of forests being felled on reclaimed farms for the quick cash boost of selling the timber. He talked of violence and intimidation.

Local thugs had prevented Janie from voting in the recent farcical presidential elections which nearly all international inspectors decried. As the South African delegate took the stand and delivered his verdict of 'a free and fair election' the hall erupted in disgusted laughter and many inspectors walked out. It is to South Africa's shame that they have supported Mugabe's actions by simply refusing to denounce them. More than any other country, South Africa should be alert to the implications of this slippery slope.

Janie was an honest, hard-working man, and entertaining company. Arno asked him what he thought could be the solution for Africa. Why was the majority of this wonderful continent mired in poverty, disease and corruption. Janie replied, wearily, "You guys are going to think I'm a bloody racist, but when I get up there (points to Heaven), I will say to the good Lord, 'Why on earth did you make the African?'"

I was sorry to hear this response and, over the next few months, sadly came to realise that it was not only the likes of Robert Mugabe and right-wing white extremist Eugene Terreblanche who still saw things in simple black and white.

Mutare to Cape Town

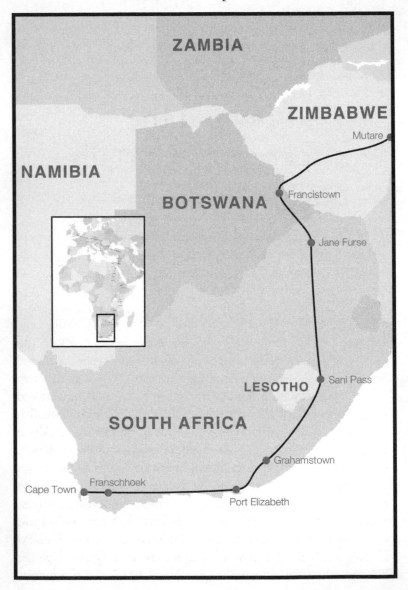

Behind the
Boerewors Curtain

We shall not cease from exploration,
And the end of all our exploring
Will be to arrive where we started,
And to know the place for the first time.
TS Eliot

South Africa immediately felt different to the rest of the continent. It was wealthy, developed, dangerous and fascinating. My first concern was that finding places to sleep would be difficult: land was all privately fenced off and staked with instructive pictures of handcuffs, dogs and rifles. Stealth, and a bit of cheeky fence jumping, was in order for me. Alone once more, and in the new atmosphere I sensed in South Africa, I felt more scared about camping than I had for months. I was disgusted at myself as I realised that even just a few days in South Africa had given me, despite all my time in Africa, an us-and-them mentality. I felt vulnerable and I felt white. So I hid carefully in thorny bush where nobody could see me. Piebald clouds across the full moon reminded me of a similar night in Ethiopia. I wondered whether Sarah was looking at the moon.

A pick-up truck (*bakkie*) pulled over one day and a couple invited me to their home for lunch, and I gratefully accepted. Hennie Kruger was about thirty years old, huge, blond, sun-weathered and wearing very, very tight khaki shorts, a khaki shirt and knee length socks. His wife, Margie, had a blow-dry perm with cheap highlights, gold stud earrings and showed ample signs of enjoying their five barbecues, *braais*, each week. They were classic Afrikaners. Afrikaners are the 'white tribe' of South Africa, descendants of the Dutch, and integral to the life and history of South Africa. Hennie told his wife to make us some lunch and she obediently toddled off towards the kitchen. Smiling in anticipation he told me he had just made a fresh batch of *boerewors*, a long curly sausage ubiquitous in South African outdoor eating. He happily talked me through the ingredients to whet our appetites.

We were sitting on the veranda, sheltered from the sun and wind by a row of tall poplar trees. Their child, a solid six-year-old replica of Hennie, ran barefoot round the garden shouting and fighting whole armies of imaginary foes. Hennie spoke in thickly accented and rarely used English (Afrikaans and Sotho were his dominant languages) of his deep love for the farming life and the peace and quiet of the bush. He had not been into town for three months. He spoke about rugby, *braais* and blue skies, the passions of virtually all white South African men. Our twenty minutes of idle chat before lunch included a biblical explanation of why black people are inferior to white people, and why it is wrong for blacks and whites to mix.

South Africa is working very hard to rebalance itself. White South Africans have been brought up for generations ignoring the obvious unpleasantness and unfairness of their country and it is hard to change ingrained dogma. I encountered little racism amongst the younger generations of urban whites and I hardly ever encountered racist blacks. Mandela's dignified forgiveness set the benchmark for his Rainbow Nation to aim for in the early 1990's when violent revolution was a very real possibility. Archbishop Tutu's Truth and Reconciliation hearings provided amnesty and a new beginning in exchange for honesty and repentance of apartheid-era crimes. The emphasis was on forgiveness and working together for a happier future.

Today *Affirmative Action* is fast-tracking blacks in all walks of life, a necessary phase on the long walk to establishing justice in South Africa. That the population is predominantly black means that the best person for a job will usually be black anyway, but this period of redressing the balance is hard on young whites looking for jobs and promotion and many have left South Africa. After a decade of democracy, there is now something of a homecoming revolution. People are returning to South Africa, trying to make it work and focusing on the good news, of which there is a great deal. South Africa has had to wash her dirty laundry in public, yet all countries have race issues. South Africa is dealing with hers more openly than most. Crime and violence felt more tangible in South Africa than most other countries in Africa, yet it is one of the few African examples of a functioning government, infrastructure and economy. South Africa has its problems, but every other country on the continent would enjoy its democracy, economy and potential.

Reaching South Africa was special for me not only because it was the final country in Africa, but also because it was a country I knew. After leaving school I came and taught for a year in a little rural school, before I went to university. Nelson Mandela had just become President and South Africa had won the rugby World Cup. The country was awash with optimism, and hopes were deliriously high for the future. It was a good time to be in South Africa.

I had lived in Lebowa, one of the 'Homelands' of the apartheid era. The apartheid governments ('half-baked dreamers with a nasty streak', as John Simpson described them) turfed countless black families out of their homes in fertile 'white areas' and crammed them together in arid, barren wastelands rebranded as semi-autonomous Homelands. Despite its aridity, Lebowa was beautiful. The land was covered with koppies and the earth was red and dry. Like tomatoes on a market stall the vast red boulders of the *koppies* were piled into enormous pyramids. Amongst them leathery green aloes grew. Skinny cattle wandered the balding earth. Burned out carcasses of vehicles were dotted around, relics of the vicious 'taxi wars' of the mid 1990's between rival groups of minibus taxi owners When I arrived in the village of Jane Furse, fresh from school, in 1995, the walls of the market were scarred with bullet holes and angry graffiti shouted 'Welcome to Beirut'. Now, after six years, I was riding back to Jane Furse.

I passed through the town of Lebowakomo and was delighted to see that the fellow who used to run a public call booth by tapping into the main phone line had still not been arrested. A panel beater seemed to be branching out: his rough hand-painted sign read 'penile biter'. I was an impatient rider: the distances had never seemed so great when I was travelling round by minibus. But eventually I arrived back in the village of Jane Furse. 'Mokoko's Fried Chicken' was still there, the dirty fast food place I had never dared enter in my gap year but which now looked quite appealing. There is nothing like returning to a place that remains unchanged to find the ways in which you yourself have altered. I was back on familiar ground for the first time since Yorkshire!

I dismounted and walked down the hill to the school, partly to savour the moment and partly because my brakes didn't work. I smiled and smiled. Past the minibus taxi rank, still pumping with deafening music distorted through cheap speakers. Big ladies were still sitting by the road selling bananas and cool drinks to the taxi passengers. As usual my passing generated hilarity and curiosity. But in Jane Furse I was not quite so much of a stranger. I knew where I was going. I surprised people as I wheeled my bicycle through the busy street by greeting them in Sotho, "Dumela, Ma! Agee? Legae! Rekona legae!" "Hello, Ma! Good morning, how are you? I'm very, very well!" It was good to be back: I felt comfortable. That village did so much for me. It was there that I fell in love with Africa, there that I first dreamed of seeing some of the world. I had wanted to return for years and finally I was back.

Riding south I camped in the garden of an Afrikaans farming family. Their bungalow was simply furnished with fading furniture. The walls were flaking and needed a coat of paint. The parents were not well educated but the nine-year-old daughter was a precocious 'new' South African, happy to chatter in Afrikaans, English or Zulu. She helped her parents with English words as they asked me about life in England. The Afrikaans farmers are tough folk, working ferociously hard to keep themselves afloat, and casting increasingly anxious glances at Zimbabwe's lunacy. They were good people and they filled me up on pap (the latest name for the dense corn-meal porridge resembling mashed potato that had been the staple diet since it was called ugali back in Kenya), fried eggs and cups of tea. I spent about an hour in the night chasing their Jack Russell around the garden, trying to stop it from throttling the cat who squealed in anguish every time the dog got her by the windpipe. In the morning I was told that was how they always played. In South Africa even the pets are tough.

The Free State region is notorious for long, flat monotonous roads. In my experience though they are long, hilly and monotonous. In a car you wouldn't even notice the gradients as you zoomed along half asleep, steering wheel gripped between your knees and pie crumbs scattered over your lap. But on a bike each climb hurts. I enjoyed the Free State. It was a province of massive skies, yellow grass, creaking old irrigation windmills, roll after roll of pale fields and occasional farms snuggled inside clusters of dark green trees. Nelson Mandela loved it too for its big skies and calm. The farmers were reserved but kind and the days and miles rolled by. I asked a man leaving his home for directions. After setting me right he called back into the house in Afrikaans then departed in his car. His wife emerged with a plate of ice cream cake for me, smiled and returned inside. I left the licked-clean plate by the gate and a note with my limited Afrikaans:*"Dankie! Lekker!"* ("Thanks! Excellent!")

At nightfall one evening, I had found no camping spot and there was no wild land around where I could camp. I didn't want to knock on someone's door after dark, so I sneaked stealthily into a small private wood close to a farmhouse. I very quietly pitched my tent, ate and settled down for the night, hiding from the two potential foes: wild, rampaging axe murderers whose sheer improbability did not deter me from hiding carefully from them each night, and the far less improbable irate landowners, wielding shotguns. I was back on the road again before dawn. Finding a safe, hidden campsite was a daily challenge on my journey. I rarely worried once I was settled in whatever hideout I found for the night, unless I heard voices or slamming car doors nearby. Then I would lie tense, alert and wide awake, listening for heavy breathing, creeping footsteps approaching, and the distinctive sound that sharpening a blood-crusted axe blade makes. I always made sure that nobody saw me sneak from the road into the wood or ditch where I intended to sleep. I kept quiet, kept my head down and my ears open. I kept my laughably small knife beside my head, as a desperate last resort.

As I began to see the flat-topped Drakensberg mountain range far ahead, still small by the hand of distance, my band of tarmac seemed to be leading me straight towards the highest of the peaks. I had turned down a generous invitation of accommodation from a luxury hotel received through my website, in order to make a detour for my final challenge: riding over the highest road in Africa. Foolish? Perhaps, but as Eddy Mercx said, "There are no laws that govern the will." Sometimes "the heart has its reasons that the head knows nothing of". The climbs grew more severe as I approached Lesotho. The border officials were friendly, but punishing mountains rose ahead. Far across the fields a shepherd, swathed against the cold in a blanket, wellington boots and a conical straw hat, sang to himself and the tune carried gently through the still air.

Light seeped from the pale sky as I pitched camp outside a small electricity substation. Camping there ensured that I had my own personal guard for the night. In true African style the night watchman of the station, Simon, was not doing much guarding and was busy listening to a lot of static and not much music on his radio. I gave him some batteries to tide him through the long night. He had been trying to recharge his old batteries by heating them on a gas ring. I lay in the cold tent awaiting the explosion.

Lesotho is a high mountainous land, far from any ocean. The climbs never stop and the gradients can be up to 35%, so steep that even pushing the bike turned me into a sweaty, collapsed heap lying beside the road. Day after day of extraordinary mountain passes. Each climb took a few hours of hard effort, clawing higher, metre by precious metre, knowing that as soon as the summit was reached then gravity would continue its punishment, laughing evilly, as it whisked me all the way back down to the valley floor to start again. The descents were lethally steep hairpin bends that I had to slalom zigzags on to try to keep my speed down as my brakes no longer worked. I wore a hole through the sole of my left shoe dragging it along the ground. Up, down, up, down, up, up, up. My bike was in a terrible state with broken spokes and no brakes. I had to manually change gear with an old toothbrush, my rack was spliced with string and a spoon and the inner tube stuck out through a tear in the tyre. My back wheel was so wobbly that Rita could no longer freewheel. Each day I endured punctures through my tired tyres and my worn chain kept snapping. With Cape Town only weeks away I no longer cared about the bike, just so long as it got me there. My clothes were as tattered as my bike and I must have looked like a tramp on wheels. My mind and my spirit were almost running on empty too. Tiny incidents would waft me to tears or triumph. My thoughts disappeared into an empty black void of confusion if I tried to contemplate anything beyond Cape Town, so I didn't bother. I just thought all the time of getting to Cape Town.

I had hoped to spend a night in a diamond mine, but I arrived after the gates had closed for the night, so I ended up in the pub owner Anthony's backroom instead. It was dark when I pushed open the creaking corrugated tin door of the shebeen in a windswept shanty village of furtive shadows and pariah dogs. I saw drunken silhouettes outlined in the dim light from smoky paraffin wicks burning in old beer bottles. The air inside was warm, smoky, alcoholic and sweat tainted, a thick contrast to the sharp and cold night. Despite his astonishment at my appearance, Anthony was more than happy to assist.

He showed me to a metal shed. Outside a pack of growling guard-dogs prowled, and Anthony advised me to stay inside until daylight. Even in all my clothes, sleeping bag and three borrowed blankets I was cold throughout the night. Yet when I woke in the morning I felt for the first time that in fact I didn't want to arrive in Cape Town. My life was so settled: I knew my routine. I knew what I was doing today and tomorrow and next week. Cape Town meant uncertainty and big decisions. In Cape Town I had to think whether or not to continue the ride. And if I did continue then I needed to find a way to get across the Atlantic. I had no idea how to even begin figuring that one out. So I tried to just enjoy today.

A sure sign that I was not the first foreigner to pass this way was every small child yelling at me for sweets. I shouted "SWEEEEEEEEETS!" back at them and confused them. Happy mayhem: this felt like good old Africa again after the quietness of South Africa. Poverty and barefoot begging and pandemonium in the markets. Mealie (corn-on-the-cob) sellers wafted small piles of glowing charcoal with squares of cardboard. Pulses of blue smoke mingled with the crowd as the yellow cobs slowly browned. I realised how quickly the wealth and infrastructure of South Africa had made me forget what most of Africa was like: wonderful but exhausting. Minibus taxis swerved amongst shoppers whilst stall owners sat quietly waiting for business beside their wares.

A teenager played a guitar made from a cooking oil tin. His tune was upbeat as I pedalled through his village heading towards ever tougher mountains. It was good to realise that I hadn't totally lost my enjoyment of the ridiculous. I was 3,200 metres above sea level by mid-afternoon and I still had another two mountain passes before I reached the highest. I rode up towards the source of a sprightly trout stream, its cool water a delicious temptation and in a grove of willows I submerged my hot, throbbing head. "Clear, clean chill currents coursing and spuming through the sour and stale compartments of the brain, bleared eye sockets, filmed tongue." The air was awash with a heady fragrance. Was it rosemary? Perhaps thyme? I would have liked to have had somebody to ask. The valleys far below me blushed with pink blossom. Outside every small round home grew a bright pink cherry tree. Blankets were hung outside to air in the sun, heavy lurid squares depicting teddy bears, kitsch flower arrangements or improbable mountain-scapes. Blue mountain ranges flowed over each other, an ocean of incredible beauty in all directions. As Paul Theroux appreciated, the silence was so great that it was nearly visible.

I could barely push the bike up the roads, let alone cycle. My arms and my legs and my back hurt. I listened to Pie Jesu on my headphones. The only disturbance to its languid grace was my rapid, ragged breathing flecked with saliva and exhortations to myself of, 'come on, Al, just a little farther, Al, always a little farther.' Every pedal stroke improved the view but diminished how much I cared. There was an overwhelming sunset as I eventually crested the summit of the Tlaeeng Pass. At 3,275 metres this was, at last, the Highest Road in Africa. It was all downhill from here. A jackal darted across the road. It would soon be dark. It was very cold. I was hungry. I was racing along alone with absolutely no idea of where I would sleep, no idea where I would find something to eat and no idea who I would meet next. A slow sunset silhouetted all before me, ridge after ridge of wild, empty mountains. Below me the hills were a hundred shades of green, with the exception of one hillside glowing with red heather.

If the journey needs defining snapshots, that pass epitomised why I began the ride. Douglas Coupland's *Generation X* asks: 'What one moment for you defines what it's like to be alive on this planet? What's your 'takeaway'?' I began because England was too easy. "The days were not full enough, and the nights were not full enough, and life slipped by like a field mouse not shaking the grass." I wanted something that I did not know that I was capable of. I would never know unless I tried. I wanted unpredictability. I wanted to demand more of myself than I could demand from others. I wanted open space. I wanted anxiety and insecurity, storm and strife, even if I did not always have the courage to cope with them. I wanted to strive, to seek and to see whether or not I would yield. I wanted to overload my senses. I felt that I would only know my strength if I took the strain, that I needed to taste blood to know I was hurt, needed to be thrashed by a gale to accept it was windy, needed to taste lung to believe I had pushed myself hard. I needed to confirm that I was alive. That day all Africa lay beneath me. When Edmund Hillary reached the summit of Mount Everest he declared: 'Well, we knocked the bastard off!' Now I knew a fragment of how he felt.

Ordinarily with sporting events and expeditions there are defining moments, celebrations and opportunities to reflect. The Tour de France is three weeks long, climbing Everest or sailing round the world may take three months. But I had been on the road for over a year and had not even made it through Africa yet. I had years more of all this ahead of me. So I found it hard to grasp a sense of perspective because I had little idea of what lay ahead of me, of how long the journey would take, or how difficult the challenges ahead may be. I never knew what would be the overall significance of each particular milestone I reached. There was never time to relax and bask because as soon one peak was reached a whole new horizon of challenges, obstacles and logistics opened up in front of me. So I climbed back on my bike and free-wheeled down the road.

REPUBLIC OF SOUTH AFRICA
AMENDMENT OF
TEMPORARY RESIDENCE PERMIT

The Temporary residence permit on

on page 20 is hereby extended until

11-01-2013

Indifference or Despair

Despair is a narcotic. It lulls the mind into indifference.
Charlie Chaplin

I dropped down the Sani pass from Lesotho back into South Africa. Descending the pass was frightening: a series of tight hairpin bends with carcasses of careless vehicles sprawled on their backs in the gorge below, a grisly reminder to keep concentrating. Only 4WD vehicles could attempt the road. Tourists are driven up the pass in special tour groups and I grinned smugly at their surprise when they saw me. I am so vain sometimes. The distinctive peaks of the Drakensberg with names like Giant's Cup and Devil's Knuckles stood tall above the quaint old towns of Underberg and Himeville. I rode across Kwa Zulu Natal amongst prosperous, English-speaking farms. Leaving Kokstad I climbed a pass and on the far side was the Transkei, another of the former semi-autonomous Homelands of the old South Africa.

There were no smart farmhouses in the Transkei. The landscape was instantly much poorer. Mud huts, potholes, cows on the road, trampled fences. Women sold individual cigarettes and matches to passers-by. Clusters of youths loafed around with nothing to do today or tomorrow: no work, no escape. There was an air of surliness that I had not felt in most of Africa. Unemployment was almost absolute in the Transkeihe only hope was to seek work in the big cities. Often men would not return home to their families for a whole year. A whole year saving pennies. Lines of young men sitting on the pavements in cities, hoping to be picked up for a day's unofficial labour here and there. Boys standing on streets at all hours guarding cars or begging at traffic lights in the hope of a small reward.

I had been bombarded with warnings about theft, murder and the general nastiness of the Transkei. Nobody had a good word to say about the area, which was often described as 'cruel'. A few people thought that I should take a bus or arrange a police escort through the area. Some white people would not drive through the region let alone cycle. I didn't know whether it was white paranoia, genuine danger or a bit of both, but I would soon find out. To be on the safe side, I made a point of staying with village chiefs each night.

One night I stayed in the chief's office in a small village near Qumba (pronounced in two syllables as '*click*-umba'). His village was a cluster of conical, thatched mud huts painted turquoise. Only half of each house was painted so that the sun would heat the unpainted area and keep the home warm into the night. After apologising for not speaking Xhosa, I explained my journey, as so often before, through a squirming, embarrassed teenager who could speak English. I explained that I was completely self-sufficient: everything that I needed was in my panniers. I did not need anything except the chief's permission to stay and his assistance to find me somewhere safe to pitch my tent for the night. "Of course you can stay!" he replied. "You can stay right here!" And he spread his hands wide to encompass the very hut we were talking in. Despite my protests of self-sufficiency I spotted four ladies pooling their money to buy a small square of margarine for my supper.

In the morning, the chief's youngest son came to my hut with a basin of hot water for me to wash with. He walked carefully across the dew-pearled grass, tongue out and concentrating hard not to spill the water. I ate breakfast with the chief at his desk. His wife served us bowls of sour brown porridge. I had never acquired much of a taste for the various breakfast porridges of Africa but I was at least well practised by now in the art of politely eating anything I was served. Porridge is, as HW Tilman wisely noted, at least a convenient way of conveying to your mouth large quantities of sugar. Over bread, margarine and tea from chipped cups he told me about his busy day ahead rectifying a cornucopia of local disputes. The chief was caring, welcoming and sensible. What else should you expect from Nelson Mandela's own people?

Despite the safe havens I was welcomed into each night, I was still on edge, tendon tight, a quivering rope beyond its safe strain limit. Perhaps it was the stark warnings I had been battered with. Perhaps it was the underlying hopelessness I sensed in the region. Perhaps it was my body and mind crying out for a break, my heart and nerve and sinew almost gone. I was determined not to grow indifferent but after almost a year of Africa's struggles I could not bear any more. Despite the positive evenings I spent the days riding with a denial of music in my headphones ('...Doctor what is happening to me? Palpitations, my mind is diseased...' sang James). I just wanted to get to the end. I set about learning the Xhosa for 'Sod this, I want to go home.' (*'Rha ndifuna ukugoduka'*: easier done than said.)

I felt more attached to South Africa than any other country and I cared about its future. I wanted to fill myself with positive images of the country but I could not do it in the Transkei. I was tired, numb and, though I don't think I realised it, scared by the potential savagery. There was no way I was carrying on after Cape Town, I resolved. The emotional oscillations were still in full swing. England to Cape Town. England to Cape Town. England to Cape Town. There was a nice ring to that. Yes, I was definitely packing it all in at Cape Town.

The End of the Beginning

This is not the end. It is not even the beginning of the end.
But it is, perhaps, the end of the beginning.
Winston Churchill

The brown hills were once more dotted with green aloes and bushes. The land grew less barren; the end of the Transkei was approaching. I was weaving amongst wide, winding rivers closing in on the sea after their long journeys. I passed a signpost for Coffee Bay. Back in Malawi I had met a German on a motorbike on a bridge. He had told me that Coffee Bay was his favourite place in Africa. I suddenly remembered his advice and decided to take a left and check it out. It was a beautiful, windy, winding ride to Coffee Bay up and down steep-edged river valleys, the landscape crumpled like a screwed ball of paper. Angry black clouds highlighted the lush green of the hills. Splashes of blue hung in the sky. A spear of sunlight struck a field, gilding it. The wind gripped and dragged the grinding, churning clouds across the sky. I had not seen the ocean since Tanzania. Reaching the cliff tops I hid my bike in some bushes and went for a walk. The wet, shining grass was warm under my bare feet and I breathed in the smell of the sea and the moist green hills of the gorgeous Wild Coast. I climbed higher, up a steep, grassy slope on the edge of a cliff. It was good to be alone once again, away from the endless watching eyes of the crowded Transkei, away from having to watch my own back. The green sea stirred milky as waves crept in and crashed. Dolphins gently rose and fell, their shape clear below the green water. Massive waves boomed as cows daintily nibbled the very edge of the bluff. I felt my mind relax, the knots and tightness massaged free by the lonely sea and the sky with the white clouds flying. You cannot find silence beside the sea. After the Transkei and my vagrant gypsy's life it was just what I needed.

Leering youths in Butterworth made throat-slashing gestures at me as darkness fell and I struggled to repair a puncture. Stupidly I gave them the finger and then pedalled like mad to get out of town and find somewhere to hide and camp. The next day I rode through King William's Town, the home of one of my first South African heroes, Steve Biko. Biko was the founder of the Black Consciousness movement and one of apartheid's most famous martyrs. He was the subject of the film *Cry Freedom*. I enjoyed his feistiness, for example his famous argument with a judge in one of his many court appearances: "Mr. Biko," asked the judge, wearily, "Why do your people insist on calling yourselves 'black'? To my eye you are more brown than black?" "Your Honour," Biko replied, "why do your people call yourselves 'white'? To my eyes you are more pink than white." The judge was not amused.

I camped in a grove of aloe trees. Yellow and purple flowers, aloes, cacti and a winding brown river spread across the wide depths of the Great Fish River Gorge. This was the river described in Rian Malan's book, *My Traitor's Heart,* as the old white man's frontier. The land from the Cape to here was well known to early European settlers but beyond this river lay the dark, frightening unknown stretching on endlessly towards Cairo. I was on the finishing straight now.

Grahamstown had the feel of an English market town. It is famous for its churches, schools, university and an annual arts festival. Streets were edged with puddles and trees blowing in the mad, random wind. It felt like home. I had come to Grahamstown to talk about my ride at some schools. I was walking through town with my bike one morning thinking how something as ordinary and familiar as a High Street becomes fascinating when seen out of context when I was startled by somebody sprinting across the road at me, waving his arms and shouting "Al! Al! Al!" The excited stranger set about calming my rather alarmed face. I was happily surprised as Simon Schoon explained that he had been following my progress down Africa on my website and had been thinking just that morning that I was now probably somewhere close to Grahamstown. We had coffee in a café and chatted.

I quickly liked Simon: he had a great enthusiasm for life and an appreciation of the ridiculous. He was really eager to help me, especially after looking in horror at the terrible state poor Rita was in. The bike shop he took me to was also excited by my journey and incredulous about my bike, insisting on repairing the brakes and changing the tyres free of charge. While the mechanic worked Simon took me to Rhodes University, where he was studying, so that I could use the internet. The internet was an invaluable tool during my journey, allowing me to email my family regularly to reassure them (or remind them) that I was still alive, to research and plan my route, to keep up to date with Leeds United and other key global issues, and to update my website. My website was useful for promoting *Hope and Homes for Children* and for telling a wider audience about my journey which brought me assistance from strangers in many parts of the world. The website also added a veneer of professionalism and focus to my ride, which otherwise may have appeared to be rather bumbling. This helped at times where people needed to be impressed by hard evidence and facts rather than by word of mouth, trust or imagination, for example when I was trying to arrange speaking engagements or interviews or to wangle free passage across oceans. Finally, updating my website was something that I enjoyed for my own pleasure, spending large amounts of time on the road pondering how I would try to portray a particular country in just a few brief sentences.

Bike fixed, website done. Pub beckoned.

We sat in the 'Rat and Parrot' pub with some of Simon's friends, Vicky, Kirsty and Paul. As the table slowly disappeared beneath empty glasses I felt a deep melancholic happiness, enjoying the reminder of nights of laughter with like-minded, adventurous friends. Alcohol and chaste months combined to turn every woman into a beautiful Siren and I grinned stupidly at the world until the bar staff had wiped down the last table and booted us out into the night.

After all the recent rain the hills were lushly green and clouds scudded high in the warm wind. A group of boys from St. Andrew's school accompanied me on their bikes for 5 miles out of Grahamstown and Simon, Kirsty and Paul continued another 25 miles with me. They waved me off after we had all written our names on a road sign, inspired presumably by similar sentiments to David Livingstone carving his initials on trees during his travels.

A wearing side to my ride was being asked exactly the same questions every single day by every single new person I met. I always enjoyed being able to stay with a family for more than a couple of days because then I was able to chat about things other than my bike ride. People's curiosity was always on similar lines: "Did you get sick? What was the worst thing that happened to you? What was your favourite place? Wasn't the ride dangerous? Doesn't your bum hurt?"

I always tried to remind myself that for everyone I met it was the first time they had asked 'The Questions' and that they were perfectly normal questions to ask. I remembered Ffyona Campbell's rude attitude to the drip torture of 'The Questions' in her books and promised myself that I must be courteous. The urge to become sarcastic grew ever stronger though as the days, weeks and months piled up. At times I would go through phases of deliberately avoiding people as I could not bear to explain myself yet again. The Questions came thick and fast, often with no greeting to begin the process, giving me no time to escape or to ask any questions of my own.

"Where have you come from?"

"England."

218

"That is your country. Where have you come from on your bike?"

"England."

"No, that is too far. Where have you come from on your bike?"

"England."

Sceptical looks and a change of tack.

"But how do you cross the oceans? Do you pedal very fast over the water?" (Ha!Ha! How I laughed at this annoyingly regular favourite. It wasn't even funny the first time.)

"Why are you alone?"

"I have no friends."

"What is your job?"

"This is my job."

Many questions revolved around my perceived wealth. I became good at fending these off, though I dreaded them more than any others and my heart would sink when a newly made friend started to care only about my bank balance.

"How much does this cost, my friend? And this? And this? And this? Perhaps you will be giving me your sunglasses?"

When questions focused solely on money I felt like an outsider, a circus show, a freakish demonstration of outrageous Western wealth. The people I liked most were the people who did not care how much my shoes cost and had deeper interests in my life and my journey and the coincidental brief crossing of our lives.

"How much do you earn in England?"

"Well, a packet of cigarettes in England costs the same as twenty packets here, and a room in London costs £500 a month so it is a very expensive country to live in."

"How did you afford your journey? Are you very rich?"

"I saved some money and now I live very cheap. I spend less every day than a sandwich costs at home. I sleep in my tent and I eat lots of bananas."

"How much is your bike?"

"About 50kg." (A great deflection).

"Where are you going to?"

"Today I am going to the next town, about 100 kilometres away."

"You are going there, on a bicycle! You are crazy! Do you realise how far that is? It is 100 kilometres from here! You are crazy! It is not possible!"

"Bye bye."

After another bruising battle with the wind, so strong it seemed to dent the balls of my eyes, I made it to Jeffrey's Bay. J-Bay is the surf Mecca of South Africa. I had wanted to go there ever since I discovered that the perfect wave immortalised in the film *Endless Summer* was just around the corner. Disappointingly J-Bay had none of the wandering, dream-chasing spirit of that endless summer and had contented itself with becoming a shoppers' paradise for out of shape Brits on their fortnight's break from office routine. In their new *Billabong* and *Quiksilver* clothes they at least looked the part. I propped up a beach bar and marvelled with the barmen, in that unattractive male way, at one of the most captivating bikini girls that we had ever (in our collective wisdoms) had the good fortune to set eyes on. She was so stunning that none of us dared to even go and say hello as she sat alone and bored. Oh, the unspeakable tortures of being a tongue-tied, average-looking male.

I do not know what provoked me, but for some reason I decided to thrash out over a hundred miles into the wind to the village of Plettenberg Bay. The thrill of pushing hard, the joy of realising that you can do it, of knowing that you have taken something on and pushed against your personal barriers to achieve it is electric. My legs and body were weak and feeble but my mind was fired with life. With the sun close to the black hills and angling into my eyes I rounded a corner and below lay Plettenberg Bay. I had a rush of pride. "I've done it! I've beaten this damn continent!" I screamed down the pass, adrenalin roaring through my body as I slashed the corners tighter and faster and shouted and shouted in triumph.

Tired yet smiling I pulled into the village. Offshore, Southern Right Whales broached to shrieks of delight from binocular-clutching admirers. This suited me as I could lie in the grass, eyes closed against the sun, and just sit up and enjoy the whales' appearances whenever the whooping started.

But the real bonus of reaching Plett was that I bumped into the bikini girl once again. To my complete surprise she approached me and even spoke to me. She was travelling along the Garden Route for a few weeks holiday and was going to stay in Plettenberg Bay for a few days. Suddenly I was not quite so desperate to reach Cape Town. What difference does a few days make, I reasoned.

"Where have you come from?" she asked.

"England!" I beamed heroically.

"That is your country. Where have you come from on your bike?"

"England!" flashed from my most charming smile.

"No, that is too far. Where have you come from on your bike?"

"What a superb question! Would you like to have a coffee whilst we discuss it?"

"But how do you cross the oceans? Do you pedal very fast over the water?"

Once I had calmed down from my waves of delighted laughter at this most hilarious and original joke, I explained modestly how I had swum the channel in only my briefest of Speedos, wrestling sharks and rescuing a young child or two along the way.

"Why are you alone?"

"Travelling alone is a chance to look deep into my soul and to write poetry, because long-distance cycling is not just about having muscular thighs and sculpted buttocks." (I flexed my legs to demonstrate that, despite being sensitive and thoughtful, I was also well honed.) "Above all, I chose to travel alone because maybe, just maybe, I would meet a special and wonderful soul mate somewhere along the road. Perhaps you would like to try on my sunglasses?"

And on and on rolled my nonsense, and my head span with the delirious novelty of flirtation and the waiter was exhausted as he brought coffee after coffee and piles of cakes that I didn't want and couldn't afford but I didn't care just so long as I could keep this girl beside me.

The final question came: "Where are you going to now?"

"I thought I might hang around here for a few days: I hear they have a fascinating village museum…"

"Oh I am so glad. I am staying by the beach. Why don't you come with me?"

At times I loved the attention that my bike got me.

"Surely the Franschhoek pass must be the final pass in Africa?" I panted to myself some days later. Around me the hills were covered in *fynbos* heather, looking like a sunny day in Scotland. Rocky outcrops separated noisy brown streams. I clung to a scrap of shade beneath an overhang to write my diary. I enjoyed my final piece of chewing gum, fastidiously rationed since Ethiopia. Up a final bend and there below me lay Franschhoek. Winding out of the valley bottom was a single road, the road to Cape Town. I drank in the cool smell of pine as I swooped down the winding road. This was just silly, I thought: immaculate vineyards combed along the lower slopes, vertical craggy heights, dazzling Cape Dutch wineries, a perfect blue sky and only two days to go till Cape Town. What on earth had I been whining (not wining) for all year? It was a sign of how close I was now that topping the pass I had hoped that I may see Table Mountain for the first time. Not yet, my friend. Not yet.

My first view of Table Mountain came just before Stellenbosch. One of my main motivations through all the tough times had been the thought of how I would feel the moment I eventually rounded that last corner or crested that last hill and for the first time gazed in wild surmise on Table Mountain and the end of Africa. But, like Mandela, 'I did not linger, for my long ride was not yet ended.' I had imagined myself weeping with joy or leaping in the air but I just smiled within myself and pedalled on. Harold Pinter said that the more acute the experience, the less articulate the expression. In the circumstances then I think that I did pretty well with a quiet "Bugger me."

A Botswanan student at the University of Cape Town, Adam Alexander, had found my website many months ago and followed my progress. He was a friend of Simon in Grahamstown. As I neared Cape Town he made contact with me, invited me to stay, and was incredibly helpful organising media coverage. He also was going to ride the final two days with me. I was concerned when I saw the sleekness of his shiny yellow triathlon bicycle and eager grin. I looked down at my sun-bleached panniers and solid mountain bike frame and feared that I was in for a painful high speed ride. Fortunately, he was more than happy to trundle along at my heavily laden pace and to join me in my regular pauses to rest, take in the view and reflect that there was just one day more. What's more, Adam had a backpack full of muffins and pies. I nearly tore his arm off as he offered me, "Spinach and feta or chicken and mushroom?"

We paused on the coast near Khayelitsha, Cape Town's largest township. Three white men stopped their vehicle beside us, their bakkie festooned with fishing rods.

"If you *okes* hang about here the bloody *kaffirs* will rob you for certain."

The word 'kaffir' encapsulates apartheid and has now acquired the status of the most offensive word in South Africa. People only ever say 'kaffir' to make a statement and even then it is usually only uttered in hushed tones, except by unpleasant men stinking of brandy and Coke. I told them that I had just cycled the length of Africa, that I felt safe and that I had talked with, eaten with, enjoyed the company of and shared the homes of Africans throughout the continent. They looked at me as though I was insane and drove away. Signs along the beautiful beach warned that automatic rifles were forbidden on the beach.

Adam and I gently cruised the last few miles through the Cape Point National Park, down the peninsula that grew narrower and narrower until finally there was no further left to ride. Cape Point. Horace wrote: 'Here is the end of the map; and of the road.' The end of Africa. The end of my road.

But to pull up in a crowded car park and say 'THE END' just did not feel right. Adam shook my hand but he looked embarrassed at what a non-event the whole thing was. Like me, Adam was a sucker for sporting high drama and emotional defining moments and he recognised a non-one when he saw it. Japanese tourists were literally queuing up to take photos, squashed together at the viewpoints, and they shuffled around me as I stood trying to gather my thoughts.

Cape Point is a magnificent lick of land striking boldly out towards Antarctica as Africa refuses to surrender softly to the ocean. Looking down from the clifftop lighthouse I watched birds flying below me and in the glass-green rolling waves seals cavorted, as oblivious to the turmoil in my head as the next damn person who was going to nudge me aside so that they could take a photo of someone with white, knobbly knees, varicose veins and a tour group badge saying 'Hi! I'm Bubba.'

I hadn't spoken to Sarah since England but now it was time to make the call. I had often dreamed of calling her first to tell her that I had done it. I really wanted to share this moment with her. But the pay phone wouldn't do International Calls. I hung up disappointed. I could not muster any excitement at all. And the ice cream shop was closed.

The celebration needed rescuing. So, as Adam returned to Cape Town for the night (he decided reluctantly that he really should do a little bit of revision for his finals exams next week) I hid at the Cape of Good Hope and waited for the tourists to leave and the full moon to rise. I sat on a sand dune and enjoyed a piece of KFC chicken that a couple had given me earlier back in the car park. A gale was blowing and the daylight was ebbing. This was how my journey should end: standing alone on the beach in a feisty wind, the Southern Cross hanging bright above me, dappled clouds scurrying across the moon and shining yellow-blue waves rolling home from Antarctica around my feet. I snuggled into my sleeping bag feeling much better now that I had the end of the road all to myself. It was my road and this was my end.

I woke late with the sun already gleaming on the ocean: a perfect smiling morning. zebras, elands and blesbok were surprised to see my head popping out from underneath a bush. False Bay was calm. All that remained was the ride into Cape Town. There was not long to go now: the final puncture, the final shady tree, the final banana sandwich, the final drink of water, the final turn of the pedals, the final beat of the heart. Along the coasts of the Misty Cliffs cyclists were out enjoying their Sunday morning cruise along one of the most beautiful roads in the world. Adam pedalled out to ride the last stretch with me. There was a final steep climb up Kloofnek hill from Camp's Bay. Behind me Adam called out that it was the Last Hill in Africa. It seemed to reach halfway up Table Mountain. In the hot sunshine we rode it hard and fast. Adam told me "Only 500 metres to go!" I turned back to him and grinned.

"Let's go!"

I stood up on the pedals and hammered hard towards the summit. I wanted a final reminder of the pain, of screaming legs and rasping lungs. It was the last hill in Africa. I sprinted with everything I had. I knew beyond doubt that nothing could stop me now. 300 metres to go. A car hooted in support. 200 metres. Just a little further. Go, go, go! For the hard times and for all the good times: GO! 100 metres. Ride, ride, ride! With every drop of heart and soul. Ride! Taste the pain! Reach deep.

Below me lay Cape Town. It was my one-man winning line.

To be continued...

Recipes from the Road

Shish kebabs – Syria

Ingredients
1 cup plain yoghurt
$1/_2$ cup olive oil
2 cloves chopped garlic
1 teaspoon red pepper flakes
1 teaspoon salt
1 teaspoon black pepper
$1^1/_2$ pounds shoulder of lamb, cut into 1-inch cubes (include some fatty pieces)
8 tomatoes
12 peppers
pita bread

Method
Mix the yoghurt, oil, garlic, pepper flakes, salt, and pepper in a bowl. Add the lamb and coat thoroughly. Cover and let marinate, in the refrigerator, for twenty four hours.

Preheat the grill to high. Thread the lamb onto the thin skewers, alternating lean and fatty pieces. Thread the vegetables onto skewers. Oil the grill grate, then add the kebabs, turning until the vegetables are blistered and the lamb is browned and done to taste.

Stuff pitas with the lamb and blistered vegetables.

Chicken Paprikash – Hungary

Ingredients
2 chopped chicken breasts
1 chopped onion
1 litre of chicken broth
sour cream
paprika
corn flour
garlic
chopped ginger
bay leaf
salt and pepper

Method
Brown the chicken, onions and garlic in a little oil in a large pot. Add the chicken broth. Add lots of paprika until the broth is dark, and then add the salt and pepper, ginger and bay leaves. Simmer for 30 minutes.

Finally, add lots of sour cream, and maybe even more paprika. Serve over *spaetzel*.

Fuul – Sudan

Ingredients
Fava beans
Olive oil
Lemon juice
Salt & pepper

Method
Mash the beans as you heat them. When hot and thoroughly mashed add lemon juice, olive oil and seasoning to taste. Sprinkle with red onion.

Eat with hot unleavened bread.

Doro Wot (Red Chicken Stew) and Injera – Ethiopia

Doro Wot

Ingredients
2kg skinned chicken drumsticks or thighs
4 finely chopped large onions
3 chopped cloves of garlic
1 cup vegetable oil
$\frac{1}{2}$ teaspoon shredded ginger
$\frac{1}{2}$ cup Ethiopian spice (or crush plenty of chilli, garlic and salt with some wine vinegar and lemon juice) enough paprika to make a deep red colour for the sauce
2 cardamom pods
$\frac{1}{2}$ teaspoon cumin
$\frac{1}{2}$ cup water

Method
In a large casserole simmer the onion and garlic with vegetable oil until they are lightly brown. Add the spices and paprika, adding a little water as needed to avoid sticking. Add the chicken and simmer for about 20 minutes. Add the other ingredients and serve hot with injera.

Injera

Ingredients
400g self rising flour
200g teff flour
100g corn flour
water

Method
Mix the ingredients in a large bowl adding water to make a batter of medium thickness. Cover the bowl and leave it to ferment for 24 hours at room temperature. Cook like large pancakes in a hot frying pan. Allow to cool before serving.

Spinach Plasas – Sierra Leone

Ingredients
2 bunches chopped spinach
500g chopped smoked fish
2 onions
100g peanut butter
3 cups water
1 cup palm oil
2 very hot peppers
500g chuck beef

Method
Put the meat,water, onion, palm oil, salt and pepper in a pan and cook uncovered for 1 hour on medium heat. Add the other ingredients, stir, cover and simmer for a further 10 minutes. Serve with rice.

Fly Burgers – Malawi

One meal that I could not sample in Malawi as I was there at the wrong time was fly burgers. At the new moon vast clouds of flies hatch from the lake and as they pass over the shore it is easy to swat huge numbers of the flies with damp wicker baskets.

Ingredients
Chaoborus edulis (Malawian Lake Flies)
Banana leaves
Chopped tomato and onion
Salt

Method
Mix the flies, tomato, onion and salt together. Pat the mixture into a burger shaped patty between your hands. Wrap each burger in a banana leaf and cook on a smoky fire. Serve with nsima (see recipe for ugali above).

Boerewors – South Africa

Ingredients
2 kg chuck beef (fat and gristle removed)
1 kg thick pork rib
200g pork fat
1 tablespoon ground coriander
2 tablespoons salt and pepper
1 tablespoon nutmeg
$^1/_2$ cup vinegar
$^1/_2$ cup white wine
pork casings

Method
Mince all the meat and fat. Mix together with the other ingredients and leave for an hour. Soak the casings in water during this period. Fry a little of the mixture to try the taste. Stuff the casings with the mixture. Cook outdoors on hot coals.

Ugali – Kenya

Ingredients
Corn flour
Water

Method
Boil a pan of water. Slowly stir in cornflour over a low heat until it is as thick as mashed potato. Continue stirring for about three minutes. Serve immediately with meat or vegetable stew or sauce.

Acknowledgements

Above all I would like to thank the thousands of friends I made along the road. Without you all I would never have made it round. Without you all it would have not been worth making it round. I am indebted to you all. If I have ridden a long way it is only by sitting on the saddles of giants.

To Mum and Dad and all my family, for a lifetime of unwavering support and encouragement, I am truly grateful. To Sarah, for making the end of my road the beginning of another incredible journey. From now on we ride tandem. To my friends who did not forget me when I was far away.

Thanks also to the Wildmen for the miles and sunsets and terrible meals shared: Rob, Dave, Chris (sorry for axing you from this book!), Arno, Simon, Toby, Ruth, Paul, Owy, Fabien and the many others I rode with, Zig, Al, Will, Dunc for reminding me to laugh, the teachers, writers, adventurers and wild spirits who taught, encouraged and inspired me, all at Hope and Homes for Children for your support, Paul Deegan for making me angry enough to start all this and positive enough to finish it, all those who have emailed me encouragement from seven continents, the thousands of school students I have shared my story with for your positive energy and enthusiasm, Leah and Toby for running my website, Terry Nielsen, Dale and Ed for letting me mess around in their boats, those bold enough to sponsor me, those who have made donations to Hope and Homes for Children, the kids I met at the HHC projects

233

for your inspiration, Diccon Swann for my favourite bit of sponsorship and to Neil and Simon for stoking the fire. And, from a cast of so many, (and at the risk of accidentally omitting someone who does not deserve to be omitted) a big thank you to Adam (big thanks), Laingers and Mike in CT, Adrienne and Mike, Aigul, Alex and Sommer, all the kind Russians and Yakut who looked after us so well, Allan Rowe, Andy Kenny, Andy Vasily, Angela Beard, Anthony Aughterson, Art and Sandy, Barb and Joel, Barman and his Kyrgyz family, Bill and Rosemary Fowlds, Brian and Courtney, Buccaneers, Byrun, Cath Barr and Johnny, Caroline and Gurkan, Cheri Howland, Chris and Malin Herwig, Chris Perkins, Coffee Shack, Dale and Fran, Danie Slabbert, Daniela and Greta, Daryl and Anne Barker, Dave and Stephanie and Carlie and Olivia McGrath, David Bonnett, Dennis and Kaye, Doris and Ray, Eb Eberlein and Gwen Goodman, Elizabeth Newport, Ellie and Kiera, Esupat, Fletch, Fogie, Fran and Will, Fraser and Candice, Gary and Barbara, Gary and Katherine, Gary and Julia Neely, Guy and Biggy, Hugues Juillerat, Ian Raitt, Irvin and Janina Luker, Isaac and Eli Chavez, James Walton (in absentia), Jane, Jeanna Schieffer, Jen and Forrest, Jenny Redlin and John Johnson, Jo and Ben, Jo and Nick, Joanne and Ed Northing, John and Sharon Melrose, John Mooney, Jon and Jenny Calderwood, Jon Bartley, Kamuzu Academy, Karen Reid, Kate Hannay and John Hurley, Kelly Pham, Kevin and Andrea, Kris Ramsden, Kuki and Gilfrid, Lance (for inspiration), Lipik, the Little Sisters of Jesus, Lynne and David Hill, Magadan Catholic Church, Mark McGough, Matej and Sana and Luka, Mayoka Village, Melissa and Joel, Merrica, Michael Collins, Michitaka Nakao and family, Mike McGee, Mitchell, Nastya Butkovskaya and family, Nick and Evelyn, Nina and Sebastian, Paul and Sinead Carroll, Pawel Szalus, Pete Farlam, Pete Jones, Peterhouse, Phil Brisley, Raymond, Red Roof Guest House, Rob and Claire McKay, Saff (keep writing!) and Matt, Sara Nielsen and Nils and Laurie, Sergei, Shannon, Sheldon and Judy, Si Schoon, Sofia Crain Corcuera y familia, Sonia, Sophie and Piers, St. Mark's College and Sonia, Stephen Heath and Becky, Steve and Linda, The Andrews, The Aynsleys, The Ballards, The Bannys, The Cannons, The Capurros, The Davidsons and Nate and the Phoenix consortium, The Fitchs (two dinners in one night!), The Gooden Family, The Hasagawas, The Hawkesworths, The Heaths, The Hughes Zoo, The Johnsons, The Llorets, The Melroseshe Mitchumshe Morton Smithshe Neelyshe Neufelds, The Rebelos, The Ripleyshe Tootellshe Village Chiefs of Africa, The Wooldridges, Will Finfrock, Zhuanom and Cindy Whittaker, Walter and Rudi, Will and Kathleen Stacey.

Thanks to Jessica for all your early encouragement and for making this book far better than it would have been otherwise, and to Sir Ranulph Fiennes for inspiration and support. Thank you to all the team at Eye Books for all your hard work.

And thanks to you for reading it.

Afterword

It is more than 10 years since I took those first nervous, excited pedal strokes away from my front door. I am pausing briefly now to stop, turn around, and look back down the long road behind me. It is no exaggeration to say that setting off to cycle round the world has changed virtually every aspect of my life.

I am still surprised, proud and relieved that the 24-year-old version of myself had the temerity, chutzpah and guts to set off on that journey. It is surely an indication of how I was not destined to a life of adventure that I am, even now, continually amazed that I did it. I am proud of the young me. And I am also grateful to him, for it led me on to such an interesting decade.

I'll pick up the story after the bike ride ended. Returning home was (still is) a cocktail of contradictions and mixed emotions. I was delighted to get home again, back to my friends and those I loved. I was happy to put the hobo lifestyle behind me, the endless road, the fleeting interactions and relationships, the cheap sandwiches munched in noisy gutters. But, after being home for a couple of months, I began to struggle. My years of searching had led me to paradise. They had led me right back to where I began in the first place. Yes, it had been a cracking adventure, but I hadn't found the Meaning of Life or the elixir of happiness. And, after an extra-ordinary experience, I found an ordinary life increasingly stifling and frustrating. I had no urge (at first) to head off on more adventures. But I was less able than ever to contemplate a normal nine-to-five lifestyle. I needed a new challenge. And so I began to write.

I poured my heart and soul into writing this first book, with all the highs and lows that entails. The second book was a smoother experience. Eventually, the books were written and published and I felt ready to put the trip behind me and make a concerted effort to grow up and settle down. Over the next year or so I went through two jobs. Both were good career paths: decent wages and a smart suit; no danger, pension and gold watch in case of eventual retirement.

But it was boring, easy and unfulfilling in comparison with those years on the road. So I quit real life and walked out into the glorious uncertainty of doing whatever the hell I wanted at 9 o'clock on a Monday morning. I would be my own boss, live by my own rules, be my own arbiter and judge. I was going to spend my days doing what I loved. I was confident (a confidence forged during those years on the road) that if I was willing to work very hard, with enthusiasm, persistence and imagination, that I might be able to make a living out of doing the things that I enjoy. My confidence was also boosted by knowing how serendipitous my life was compared to so many people I had met on my travels. If my plan failed I would not starve to death. I would always be able to find another normal job. The risk did not actually seem particularly large.

And so, little by little, I have spent the last few years earning a living as an adventurer, author and speaker. Combining adventure with sharing stories has been a lot of fun. It's not all fun: I doubt there are many people who have written books who describe that anguished task as 'fun'. And the expeditions that really appeal to me are rarely fun. Selective amnesia is one of my most useful characteristics.

I have never re-read any of my books after they are published.

I am more interested in looking forwards to the next project. And I am sure there would be so much I'd like to change. Writing this Afterword I still have not felt the urge to re-read the book. For the words in this book are the best reflection of my journey seen fresh after the event, expressed to the best of my ability as a young, novice writer. I would write the tale differently now, without doubt. For, as the years have changed me, so too they have changed my perception of that journey. And, as the journey was mine and mine alone, a changed perception would change the actual journey. How long will it be before I have forgotten more about that journey than I remember? The words I wrote at the time that I wrote this book were true to me at the time. To change them would be to change the truth and that is wrong. History might be written by the victors, but I want my book to remain written by the young person who rode it and wrote it.

Has cycling round the world changed my life? One thing is sure: fulfilling an ambition and achieving something that feels personally momentous are not the keys to lifelong happiness. If being restless, questing, ambitious and unsettled was what pushed me to cycle round the world in the first place, completing the journey has only made it worse. Opening Pandora's Box has meant that everything I now do, I compare to those salad days on the road. Seen through that dazzling prism my adventures, my current highs, my fitness, my prospects, my freedom and independence, my normal everyday level of contentment and satisfaction all struggle to live up to the glory days of my mid- to late-20s. It is not all doom and gloom, rather I just set myself higher standards now in terms of happiness, fulfilment and ambition.

Something that has changed tremendously since I decided to cycle round the world is the number of people undertaking long journeys by bike. There are many styles of bicycle travel and at least as many motivations behind them. Many people have discovered bike journeys as an interesting, challenging, cheaper improvement to backpacking. Some have picked long distance cycling for a physical sporting challenge, riding across continents -head down- as fast as they possibly can. And ever more people are undertaking epic adventures by bike. It is lovely to receive emails from people dreaming of far-flung places. I always urge them to commit to action – "Begin!" The hardest part of my journey was having the nerve to start. Everything else was relatively easy after that.

There are many reasons why I set off to try to cycle round the world. Three of the strongest factors were having no idea what "proper job" I wanted to do, craving a massive adventure and wanting to be a writer. Lacking the imagination to write fiction, I therefore set off to create a story I could write. I had little idea how one became an author. I was just going to ride and to write. My ambitions were limited: I hoped only that, one day, I might eventually sell sufficient books to cover the cost of cycling round the world (£7,000). I have done that now, and more. But I am very much still learning my craft and I harbour ambitions for future exciting journeys which I hope will lead to better books in the future.

The surprise and satisfaction of successfully completing my bike ride has had a profound impact on my outlook on life. It made me realise that I was capable of far more than I had ever imagined. The ride stretched, but did not exceed, my potential. It provided a much-needed boost to my self-confidence. I hold myself to higher standards now, in all that I do and dream of doing. And it fuelled my ambition to make the most of my life, in lots of different ways. One of those has been to head off on more journeys and adventures, though no longer by bicycle. After all, I was never a cyclist. I was just a young man, short on skills, talent and cash, looking for adventure and whatever came my way. And I tell you, if you have the desire for knowledge and the power to give it physical expression, go out and explore on a bike. For those were the best days of my life, and they have opened the way to a wonderful decade since.

It will be interesting to look back again in another decade's time, to look back from the wrong side of 40 on this journey that began as a frightened, ambitious 24-year-old. One thing I suspect will remain true. That no experience in my life is likely to match up the privileged days I spent cycling round the world, living the story that you have just read.

THUNDER AND SUNSHINE

around the world by bike

PART TWO

RIDING HOME FROM PATAGONIA

ALASTAIR HUMPHREYS

Five Finger Rapids

Abridged from 'Thunder and Sunshine',
the second part of Alastair's ride

"The river's too high…"
"The river's too cold…"
"You don't have a map…"
"You'll sink if you load your bikes onto a canoe…"
"The smoke is too dangerous…"
"Five Finger rapids will get you…"
"The bears will get you…"
"The fires will get you…"
The moniker for a long-term resident of the Yukon is a 'sourdough'. It is a term used with respect. We, clearly, were not sourdoughs. We were a pair of hopeless Englishmen and we had no chance. The verdict was a red rag to a bull and we began the search for a canoe. As Mallory said, "The greatest danger in life is not to take the adventure."

Sara, a cross-country skier and sourdough extraordinaire, was hosting us in Whitehorse. She gave Dave and me a beginners' canoeing course and lots of frightening bear-avoidance advice over a two-day training run on the nearby Takhini River. We felt ready for anything, but her young brother, Erik, expressed his doubts about our competence as he helped Dave and me load the canoe on the riverbank at the bottom of their garden. "Do you think we'll make it?" Dave asked him, breezily. "I don't think so," replied young Erik.

For the next 10 days we would be far from road or rescue with no phone to call for help. It felt very liberating.

After a short while our arms grew tired and we had to stop and take a little rest. Our arm muscles were completely unaccustomed to any form of strain. Fortunately we were around the first bend and out of sight of Sara's family so they had not seen how quickly we had tired. That was the moment when we really began to enjoy our new means of transport. We appreciated then that in a canoe, unlike cycling, you can lie back and relax and, with absolutely no effort, cruise towards your destination. Huck Finn was dead right when he celebrated life on the river as 'kind of lazy and jolly, laying off comfortable all day, smoking and fishing, and no books nor study'. We set to lying back and cruising with gusto.

Yukon Ho!

Sometime on that first afternoon the current slowed, and then stopped. We had entered Lake Laberge, and it was time to start paddling again. By evening our arms and shoulders were complaining and we paddled over to a sandy beach to pitch camp. We were extremely satisfied with our progress. We had not capsized, and we had begun to find some rhythm to our paddling. Best of all, we were completely away from roads and houses and people, away from anything created by humans. This is something that can never really be achieved on a bike journey. The campsite was idyllic and safe, a curved bay of smooth grey pebbles and bone white driftwood. We camped on a ledge above the water, a breeze kept the mosquitoes at bay, the water burbled at the shore and stars of sunlight danced on the water. We had unlimited drinking water and could even rinse off with a swim before getting into our sleeping bags. Life was good and cycling suddenly seeming like an unnecessarily arduous means of transport. Paddling the length of Lake Laberge proved to be hard work and Dave quickly retracted his bold claim, expressed with enthusiasm on the first morning, that he wanted to paddle round all of the Great Lakes. Canoeing on flat water is hard work, especially paddling into a headwind. The wind grew stronger and the water turned choppy and chalk green. We were surrounded by low, forested hills, dotted with snow even now in mid-summer. Ahead of us was a denuded hillside of bare rocks like a pile of pale intestines.

We continued to paddle hard, yet futilely, into the wind. Barbed arrows of resentment lurked at my lips as tiredness mounted, pinging round my head and desperate to be released. "Paddle harder, Dave!" "Why not this way?" "I think we should turn this way." A calmer voice knew that I was just tired. Dave was trying hard, and he was probably thinking exactly the same sort of things about me. I was had doubts about Dave's levels of effort later, though, when he re-launched his evening campaign of sit-ups and press-ups. The wind continued to rise and as the waves grew and threatened to swamp us we turned the canoe and fled for the shore. We hauled the canoe high up the beach, put up our tent and settled back to wait for calm. Surrender is, at times, the better part of valour. By evening the wind had dropped, the sky cleared and we skimmed stones across the mirror-smooth lake, kicking up silver crowns along the golden road of late sunlight. The sun sinks slowly at the top of the world, noticeably slower than at the equator where darkness falls swiftly. We fancied that we could almost see the end of the lake not impossibly far ahead and we went to bed hoping for a calm morning. The next day, a few more hours paddling brought us to the end of the lake, and we celebrated as we felt the current taking hold of our boat once more, helping us back into the flowing Yukon River. After the lake we enjoyed the changing faces of the river all the more, especially as we could sit back and relax. At other times, the river was jade green and steady with strange boils of water rising and slowly swirling the surface, at times a sliding mirror. Sometimes it was shallow and jolly, you could look down and watch pebbles rush past as though they were dashing upstream, colourful time capsules, orange, grey, white and black, each one colossally old. We slipped silently over smooth blue water and silt fizzed the bottom of the boat. The river was our road, we were content on our own and confident in the wild. It was a good feeling to travel through that silence with a good friend. The only sounds were the dipping of our paddles and our aimless chat about favourite foods, favourite films and plans for future expeditions. Moose with only their heads above water swam the river ahead of us, goofy and striving with huge ears pinned back. They scrambled up the slick bank and disappeared into the undergrowth. Sometimes we saw them grazing on the banks and they paused to watch curiously as we passed. A beaver, his big head stretched out, swam for his jumbled lodge of pale branches and mud. Disturbed by our approach, he slapped the water loudly with his tail and disappeared in a dive. Shaggy bears trotted the hillsides. Bald eagles surveyed their domain and watched us from the treetops with utter indifference. From time to time we heard them screech their haunting cry into the silent sky, then soar and plummet downwards with an audible whoosh of air. Squirrels chattered displeasure at the disturbance. Woodpeckers sounded as though they were banging their heads against a brick wall. Above the water, colourful dragonflies hovered and whirred at the surface, and vanished. Beneath us the muscular salmon were racing, but they resisted all our temptations onto our trailing hooks with lures of shiny chewing gum paper, coloured bits of plastic bags, and canapés of garlic sausage. They leaped and splashed in mockery. At night we camped on islands in the middle of the river. Islands were more likely to be safe from bears and they were more fun than sleeping on the shore. Camping on an island feels like an adventure. We were revelling in our own Huckleberry Finn or Swallows and Amazons escapade. At day's end we would look for an island suitable for landing and camping on. We would point ourselves towards an island and paddle hard. Sometimes we were foiled by the strength of the current as we paddled madly, only to be whisked right on past before we reached the island's bank. There was no chance of paddling back upstream against the current so we would have to just give up and keep on floating downstream until another island came into view. Eventually bumping into an island, we heaved the canoe up the bank, set up camp, swam, fished and then cooked on a campfire. The unusually hot, dry summer had led to record numbers of wildfires in the Yukon, so we only lit fires when we were camped on small islands in the river. We knew that, even if one did get out of control, it could not spread far. We were sick of our canoeing fare: reconstituted mashed potato and coffee for breakfast, crackers and peanut butter for lunch, peanuts and Werther's Originals as snacks, and pasta with cheap but repulsive garlic sausage for dinner. We learned too late that a canoeist can carry much more than a cyclist. Weight does not make much difference to a canoe so we could have carried a far wider range of foods. Apart from the food, those campsites were superb. As Huck Finn said, rafting down the Mississippi: 'It's lovely to live on a raft. We had the sky up there, all speckled with stars, and we used to lay on our backs and look up at them, and discuss about whether they was made or only just happened... We said there warn't no home like a raft, after all. Other places do seem so cramped up and smothery, but a raft don't. You feel mighty free and easy and comfortable on a raft. 'We felt the same with our green plastic canoe and our island campsites.

We woke to a sky thick with smoke. Ash had fallen like snow on our tent in the night. We could not see the riverbank and our noses tickled with the smoke. We were approaching the main areas of the forest fires. The breeze had changed direction in the night and blown the smoke our way, and the thickness of the smoke gave us an idea of how huge the fires were. The endless cycle of lightning strikes, forest fires and re-growth are what the respected eco-botanist Sir Elton John refers to as The Circle of Life. All the land is at different stages of growth. Forest fires leave blackened, burned hillsides stripped to bare trunks like porcupine quills. Then comes a bright blush of the pink Fireweed flower. Always the first plant to grow after the flames, it is a sign of hope, like when you first notice that a bad haircut is beginning to grow out. We passed great swathes of gaudy Fireweed, the official flower of the Yukon. Next in the cycle come small bushes thriving on the lack of competition, then poplar trees grow. And then, at last, the spruce trees begin to return. Summer lightning strikes start new fires and the circle revolves once again. The seasons revolve, the waters roll on and on, and the fires bring new life to feed future flames.

Away from the road, away from the crowd, there is no need for a clock, no need to chat. The silence stood sentinel to time, a tangible presence over the endless river that ridiculed my thoughts of distance or time. The river and the silent emptiness are wed together for ever and each smooth worn, coloured pebble will outlast us all.

Quiet traders and trappers lived along the river for year upon year, until gold was found and the river flowed with men. Now, after scores of years and shattered dreams, and a handful of winners, I was following on. There were still hints of the past. The history still breathes, the stories live on, but the river runs on and on and on. I felt optimistic for the world in a place that made man's impact feel so small.

The sky darkened and rain hurtled down as the wind rose and blew strong in our faces. We had a comical debate, as lightning slashed around us, about whether we were safe or actually very unsafe in a plastic boat on a river in a thunder storm. We duly survived unzipped and, as evening approached, a roaring sound grew louder ahead. Four great chunks of rock divide the river into five rushing channels and we paddled quickly to the shore. We had reached the Five Finger Rapids. One writer described them as 'chains of reared-up and crashing waves... a vortex that swirled like a black hole in the river'.

The endless pessimists we had met had told us that the only option was to portage our canoe and gear round the rapids, or the Five Finger Rapids would be our nemesis. Two novice canoeists, especially English ones, should not run the rapids. There was, of course, only one option available to us. We made sure that everything was tightly lashed, decided that a recce would only scare us, and paddled out to the centre of the river.

We were going for it. The likely outcomes were:

1. Death. In which case we would feel very foolish.
2. Capsize and boat sinkage. Better than #1, but much more likely. I would lose everything I owned in the world, plus we would have a very long swim to Dawson.
3. Capsize but boat doesn't sink. Not the end of the world.
4. Survive intact and disprove the doubters. Doubtful.

We alternated seats in the canoe each day for variety, and that day I was in the stern and responsible for steering. We had agreed on the route we wanted to take through the rapids. We paddled swiftly into position. We headed towards the right-hand channel as we had been advised back in Whitehorse. I was nervous but excited as the noise of the rapids increased. We paddled hard and smooth and everything was running well. The river picked up speed and we were long past the point of no return. We were committed. There was no more hesitancy, no chance to draw back. We hit the rapid and I shouted, "Paddle hard!" Dave pulled hard as I paddled and kept the canoe straight. We hit exactly the route I wanted, head on to the waves. We were bouncing madly. Dave heaved away at his paddle, pulling with all his strength. I even found time for a whoop of excitement. I felt so alert and was utterly focused on keeping us on line, but each wave we bounced over sloshed into our already over-loaded canoe. We were taking on a lot of water and began to sink lower and lower until, with almost a little sigh of apology, the boat slowly tipped us in and flipped. We had almost made it through. Almost, but not quite.

The canoe was upside down but it did not seem to be sinking. Dave grinned as we grabbed hold of the trailing ropes at the front and back of the canoe. 'Almost made it!' he seemed to be thinking. We swooped downstream hanging on to our massively heavy canoe, talking quickly and planning. We tried to push the inverted canoe towards shore, swimming against it, but the river was fast and the canoe incredibly heavy. If she shipped much more water she could sink. We raced on downstream. Nobody on the planet knew where we were. We swam hard and pushed the inert canoe, trying to move towards the bank, but it was too heavy to make any impact. We floated at high speed down the middle of the river. We tried to jam the canoe against a half-sunken log to slow our progress but the smooth, fast current just hauled us quickly past, and I gashed my shin on the log for my troubles.

The water was cold and we saw a long sweeping bend ahead, about a kilometre long. The outside river bank was a sheer hillside. We would never be able to get ashore there. We had to make one massive effort to get us, and the canoe, onto the near shore before that bend. We had to get out of the cold water as soon as possible or things could turn really serious. We shouted to each other and set our sights on a bluff on the right-hand bank. It seemed as though the river may be shallow enough for us to get our feet on the bottom and make some purchase to manhandle the boat into slower waters. Time for one extra effort. It was only a couple of hundred metres away. We pulled with all our strength but the river was dragging us on and on. The long, sheer bend was rushing towards us. We were becoming cold and tired. We knew that we had to get control of this situation quickly. We just missed the bluff but behind it was a gentle eddy where the current dropped sharply. We succeeded in hauling ourselves into the eddy and we heaved the capsized boat to the shore. We managed to stumble ashore. As soon as we were out of the water, we knew that we were safe, the adrenalin subsided and the cold really kicked in. We were panting, aching, soaking wet and cold, alone on a river bank far from home. My feet were cut and bruised from hauling over the rocky bottom. But we had got the boat to shore, it hadn't sunk, we were still alive and we had made it through the Five Fingers!

We were shivering uncontrollably. My knees and jaws were chattering, my skin had turned bright red, over a pale blue undercoat. We quickly pulled gear out of the canoe, aware we needed to get ourselves warmth before hypothermia kicked in.

Some of our dry bags turned out to have been useless. Our camping and cooking gear and most of our food was soaking wet. Our bikes had been scraped along the rocks and our lucky moose skull had its teeth knocked out. Fortunately the contents of my Ark dry-bags, all the way from South Africa, were still dry, and we quickly shared out and put on all the dry clothes we had. I pulled on a horrible fluorescent green fleece that had been given to me by a commune of activists in Portland who had lived in trees to prevent them from being cut down. The fleece had belonged to somebody who had gone to Colorado to inseminate a lesbian couple he had never met. I also had a purple woolly hat given to me by an old lady in a Mormons' knitting team in Arizona. "We knit stuff for poor folks," she told me. "Here, have this!"

I quickly got a stove going to make some hot drinks while Dave set about hanging all our wet things to dry. As the sugar-loaded hot chocolate seeped down our throats and warmed our bellies, we looked at each other, still shivering frantically, and we began to giggle with delight. There was a beautiful sunset and skeins of ducks swooshed up the river past our little beach. We were hunched over with laughter, our hands still shivering wildly, spilling hot chocolate, and our stomachs ached from laughing so loud. There was delight that we had escaped from what was almost a very serious, self-inflicted situation, delight that we had been reckless enough to take on the challenge just for the hell of it, and a delight that, once again, the pessimists of the world had been overcome. We paraphrased words I once heard from Lance Armstrong, '50% of it was for the adventure, 25% of it was for ourselves, and 25% was for those who never believed.' Roll on Dawson City and a celebratory beer.

We passed through an area of forest that was still ablaze. It was an apocalyptic vision of destruction. We felt safe though, as we paddled down the middle of the river, by now about 200 metres wide and scattered with islands. The sun dimmed to a peach-coloured disc as the sky was grey with smoke. The river was grey too, as it merged with the silt-filled White River.

Visibility was almost zero. The whole world was grey. Smoke stung our eyes and noses and caught in our throats. There was no horizon and at times even the outline of the sun disappeared. It was very disorientating. No visibility, the stream slow and silent, and my nose and mouth tangy with smoke, most of my senses had been nullified. We had no idea where we were or where we were going, other than downstream. At times we had to sit still and drift, spinning gently, and allow the river to take us downstream amongst the maze of tiny islands and tangles of driftwood. Without the current we would have been lost in all the channels, but the fires were no real barrier to our progress. We wondered whether perhaps that had been all smoke and no fire.

With no map of the river, we had little idea where we were or how far remained to Dawson. It was a happy moment then one smoky afternoon as we rounded a bend and saw the small town of Dawson City hugging the right bank of the river. We paddled across, pulled alongside the bank and climbed from the canoe for the last time. We were stiff, tired and bored with our food. Yet we were thrilled to have made it, delighted to have succeeded. When people tell you that something is not possible, it is always satisfying to turn that into a positive challenge to attack with enthusiasm and optimism. We are often too liable to focus on the reasons not to do something, the excuses to take the easy option. It is easier to do nothing than to do something. It had been an honour and a delight to briefly sample a little of the exciting history of Dawson City, the gold rush and the magnificent Yukon River.

Thunder & Sunshine is the story of Alastair's journey from South Africa back to Yorkshire, via the whole of the Americas, South to North, then Siberia in winter, Japan, and back through China, Central Asia and Europe.

About Eye Books

www.eye-books.com

E ye Books is a dynamic publishing company that likes to break the rules. We publish books that truly inspire, by people who have given their all, triumphed over adversity, lived their lives to the full.

We are committed to ethical publishing and try to minimise our carbon footprint in the manufacturing and distribution of our books.

If you feel that you have a book in you, and it is a book that is experience-driven, inspirational and life-affirming, then please contact us. We are always open to new authors.

Hope and Homes
for Children

Hope and Homes for Children is a registered charity working in 13 countries in Eastern Europe and Africa. Our head office is in Wiltshire in the UK. Our Mission is to give hope to the poorest children in the world – those who are orphaned, abandoned or vulnerable – by enabling them to grow up within the love of a family and the security of a home, so that they can fulfil their potential.

Our Vision is A World Where Every Child Feels Loved.

Today, home for more than a million children in Eastern Europe is a bleak state-run institution. These children, abandoned at birth or removed from their families because of a mental or physical disability, are hidden away in facilities that rarely meet even their most basic needs.

At *Hope and Homes for Children* we believe that every child has the right to grow up with the love and care of a family. This is why we are working with governments to not only close state institutions, by moving each individual child into a caring family environment, but also to change outdated attitudes to childcare policy and practice. Closing institutions is just the beginning, not the end, and we are helping governments put in place the alternative care systems that prevent children from entering institutions in the first place.

Children who are alone due to the AIDS pandemic are being given hope. Every 14 seconds AIDS turns a child into an orphan and almost 20 million of these children live in sub- Saharan Africa. We are supporting people with HIV and families who have lost parents through AIDS. Our work keeps families together and, in the case of a parent with HIV, we help to make plans and provision for their children. We are helping to avoid the alternative: children without homes or schools, forced into begging, crime or prostitution in order to survive.

Children orphaned or abandoned through conflict are given a family and a future. In Sierra Leone, Eritrea, Rwanda and Sudan alone, there are estimated to be more than two million children orphaned by conflict. We are caring for children in parts of Eastern Europe and Africa who have been affected by conflict, war or genocide and the social disruption and poverty that result from the hostilities. These children may be living on the streets, in government camps, in local institutions or in impoverished circumstances in the community.

Should you wish to make a donation, you can do so at Alastair's own fundraising page; www.AlastairHumphreys.com. Your donation will help us to change a child's life. Whatever your contribution, it will be greatly appreciated.

To find out more about *Hope and Homes for Children*, please visit www.hopeandhomes.org

Thank you.

About the Author

Alastair Humphreys is a British Adventurer, Author, Blogger and Motivational Speaker. Aged 24, he left England to cycle round the world riding 46,000 miles across five continents and 60 countries.

More recently Alastair has walked across southern India, rowed across the Atlantic Ocean, run the Marathon des Sables, completed a crossing of Iceland, and participated in a couple of Arctic expeditions. He has trekked 1,000 miles across the Empty Quarter desert and 120 miles round the M25 – one of his pioneering 'microadventures'.

A graduate of Edinburgh and Oxford Universities, Alastair has written six books. He was named as one of National Geographic's Adventurers of the Year for 2012.

You can follow his adventures on Facebook and Twitter as well as his website www.alastairhumphreys.com